S. Hrg. 114–562

THE DAWN OF ARTIFICIAL INTELLIGENCE

HEARING

BEFORE THE

SUBCOMMITTEE ON SPACE, SCIENCE,
AND COMPETITIVENESS

OF THE

COMMITTEE ON COMMERCE, SCIENCE, AND TRANSPORTATION UNITED STATES SENATE

ONE HUNDRED FOURTEENTH CONGRESS

SECOND SESSION

NOVEMBER 30, 2016

Printed for the use of the Committee on Commerce, Science, and Transportation

U.S. GOVERNMENT PUBLISHING OFFICE

24–175 PDF   WASHINGTON : 2017

For sale by the Superintendent of Documents, U.S. Government Publishing Office
Internet: bookstore.gpo.gov   Phone: toll free (866) 512–1800; DC area (202) 512–1800
Fax: (202) 512–2104   Mail: Stop IDCC, Washington, DC 20402–0001

CONTENTS

THE DAWN OF ARTIFICIAL INTELLIGENCE

WEDNESDAY, NOVEMBER 30, 2016

U.S. SENATE,
SUBCOMMITTEE ON SPACE, SCIENCE, AND COMPETITIVENESS,
COMMITTEE ON COMMERCE, SCIENCE, AND TRANSPORTATION,
Washington, DC.

The Subcommittee met, pursuant to notice, at 2:35 p.m., in room SR–253, Russell Senate Office Building, Hon. Ted Cruz, Chairman of the Subcommittee, presiding.

Present: Senators Cruz [presiding], Thune, Daines, Peters, Nelson, and Schatz.

OPENING STATEMENT OF HON. TED CRUZ,
U.S. SENATOR FROM TEXAS

Senator CRUZ. This hearing will come to order.

Good afternoon. Welcome to each of the witnesses. Thank you for joining us. Thank you everyone, for attending this hearing.

Throughout history, mankind has refused to accept the complacency of the status quo and has instead looked to harness creativity and imagination to reshape the world through innovation and disruption. The Industrial Revolution, Henry Ford's moving assembly line, the invention of flight and commercial aviation, and, more recently, the creation of the Internet have all acted as disruptive forces that have not only changed the way we live, but have been engines for commerce that have offered consumers enormous freedom.

Today, we're on the verge of a new technological revolution, thanks to the rapid advances in processing power, the rise of big data, cloud computing, mobility due to wireless capability, and advanced algorithms. Many believe that there may not be a single technology that will shape our world more in the next 50 years than artificial intelligence. In fact, some have observed that, as powerful and transformative as the Internet has been, it may be best remembered as the predicate for artificial intelligence and machine learning.

Artificial intelligence is at an inflection point. While the concept of artificial intelligence has been around for at least 60 years, more recent breakthroughs, such as IBM's chess-playing Deep Blue victory over world champion Gary Kasparov, advancements in speech recognition, the emergence of self-driving cars, and IBM's computer Watson's victory in the TV game show *Jeopardy* have brought artificial intelligence from mere concept to reality.

Whether we recognize it or not, artificial intelligence is already seeping into our daily lives. In the healthcare sector, artificial intelligence is increasingly being used to predict diseases at an earlier stage, thereby allowing the use of preventative treatment, which can help lead to better patient outcomes, faster healing, and lower costs. In transportation, artificial intelligence is not only being used in smarter traffic management applications to reduce traffic, but is also set to disrupt the automotive industry through the emergence of self-driving vehicles. Consumers can harness the power of artificial intelligence through online search engines and virtual personal assistants via smart devices, such as Microsoft's Cortana, Apple's Siri, Amazon's Alexa, and Google Home. Artificial intelligence also has the potential to contribute to economic growth in both the near and long term. A 2016 Accenture report predicted that artificial intelligence could double annual economic growth rates by 2035 and boost labor productivity by up to 40 percent.

Furthermore, market research firm Forrester recently predicted that there will be a greater-than-300-percent increase in investment in artificial intelligence in 2017 compared to 2016. While the emergence of artificial intelligence has the opportunity to improve our lives, it will also have vast implications for our country and the American people that Congress will need to consider, moving forward.

Workplaces will encounter new opportunities, thanks to productivity enhancements. As artificial intelligence becomes more pervasive, Congress will need to consider its privacy implications. There is also a growing interest in this technology from foreign governments who are looking to harness this technology to give their countries a competitive advantage on the world stage.

Today, the United States is the preeminent leader in developing artificial intelligence. But, that could soon change. According to *The Wall Street Journal,* "The biggest buzz in China's Internet industry isn't about besting global tech giants by better adapting existing business models for the Chinese market; rather, it's about competing head-to-head with the U.S. and other tech powerhouses in the hottest area of technological innovation: artificial intelligence." Ceding leadership in developing artificial intelligence to China, Russia, and other foreign governments will not only place the United States at a technological disadvantage, but it could have grave implications for national security.

We are living in the dawn of artificial intelligence. And it is incumbent that Congress and this subcommittee begin to learn about the vast implications of this emerging technology to ensure that the United States remains a global leader throughout the 21st century. This is the first congressional hearing on artificial intelligence. And I am confident it will not be the last, as this growing technology raises opportunities and potential threats at the same time.

I look forward to hearing from our distinguished panel of experts today.

And, at this point, I'll yield to our subcommittee's Ranking Member, Senator Peters, to give an opening statement.

STATEMENT OF HON. GARY PETERS,
U.S. SENATOR FROM MICHIGAN

Senator PETERS. Well, thank you, Chairman Cruz, for calling this very important meeting.

And I'd like to thank the witnesses for taking the time, as well. And look forward to hearing your expertise on this exciting area.

You know, certainly, our Nation's history has always been defined, in my mind, by our ongoing search for the next innovation, the next big thing that's going to advance our economy and our society. Our mastery of manufacturing and automation helped the United States establish its industrial and military might.

Looking to the future, we must continue to harness this American drive to discover, to create the next big advancement, and to keep our Nation on the cutting edge. Over the last few decades, technology has changed the way we make and how we make it. Today, we boast an ever-evolving innovation ecosystem that's rooted in robotics, machine learning, and, the subject of today's hearing, artificial intelligence.

AI products like our smartphones, intelligent personal assistant, or our banks' fraud detection technology are already improving the day-to-day lives of Americans. New advances in computer processing and cloud computing are driving rapid expansion in AI development in industries as diverse as healthcare, transportation, education, and security. And they've all gone through enormous change, as all of you know.

We as a society need to help foster this broader ecosystem so we can capitalize on its benefits, including cleaner energy, new economic growth, improved safety and health, and greater accessibility for the elderly and disabled populations.

Being from Michigan, I've had the opportunity to experience firsthand the development of self-driving cars that are made possible by a combination of advanced automatic braking and lane-changing systems, cameras, sensors, high-performance computing, deep learning systems, 3D high-definition maps, and artificial intelligence.

Just last year, over 35,000 people died in motor vehicle crashes, but research suggests that about 94 percent of those accidents were the result of human error. With safe deployment, AI-fueled automated vehicles could significantly decrease this number, saving countless thousands of lives.

In addition, the World Economic Forum estimates that the digital transformation of the automotive industry alone—just the automotive industry alone—will generate $67 billion in value for the sector and yield $3.1 trillion in societal benefits before 2025. That's billions injected into our economy to boost our competitiveness, and billions saved due to major reductions in auto accident injuries and deaths, environmental degradation caused by traffic congestion and air pollution. More broadly, U.S. technology companies spent eight and a half billion dollars on AI in 2015, more than four times the amount spent in 2010. And experts predict incredible growth in the coming years in the healthcare, marketing, and finance sectors.

A critical component of this subcommittee's work is promoting and preserving American competitiveness. And, while the U.S. leads the world in investment and discoveries in AI, as we all know and as Chairman mentioned, China is quickly catching up. In 2014, Chinese scientists overtook U.S. scientists in terms of new papers published and citations of published papers in the area of deep learning, a cutting edge of AI research.

Like computer processing, nanotechnology, and biotechnology, AI has the power to dramatically change and grow the economy, but we must invest in research and in STEM education to maintain our competitive advantage. Analysts by the Council of Economic Advisors shows that doubling or tripling all research investment, something that I fully support, will allow us to continue to grow. However, targeting increases in areas of high economic productivity, like AI, may offer benefits with much smaller budgetary impact. In fact, a recent report from the White House recommends that current government spending on AI research should be doubled or even quadrupled to achieve optimal economic growth. I certainly look forward to hearing your comments on that.

We've already seen enormous gains from Federal investment in this area through NASA's work to develop AI applications for use in robotic spacecraft missions. These applications include planning, spacecraft autonomy, image processing, and rover autonomy. NASA also utilizes AI and Earth-observing satellites to optimize observations of natural disasters, like volcanic eruptions. And I look forward to hearing more about this pioneering work by NASA and the ways in which other industries have benefited from date.

And finally, while we must strive to optimize the full economic potential of AI, we must also address its potential impacts on the workforce. While new jobs will be created because of AI, we also have to think critically about the steps we can take today and in coming years to make sure that American workers are not left behind.

The Subcommittee plays a unique role in studying emerging technologies and examining ways to promote and harness scientific advancement for the greater good. I appreciate the Chairman's interest in this important issue. I look forward to working with him and continuing to advance development at AI for the greater good. And that's why I look with great anticipation to the testimony from each of you.

Thank you.

Senator CRUZ. Thank you, Senator Peters.

We'd now recognize the Ranking Member of the full committee, Senator Nelson, for an opening statement.

STATEMENT OF HON. BILL NELSON,
U.S. SENATOR FROM FLORIDA

Senator NELSON. Thank you, Mr. Chairman.

Indeed, AI has helped the space program quite a bit. I'm delighted that a representative from JPL is here. JPL are the wiz kids, the rock stars. And, in fact, they are rocket scientists.

There's another part about AI, and that is the replacement of jobs. We've got to prepare for that. For example, Elon Musk recently predicted, in an interview with CNBC, that robots could eventually take many jobs away from folks and that they would have to depend on the government in order to have a living. Elon used the example of truck drivers, who could be displaced in the future by autonomous vehicles and those kind of advancements that would allow trucks to drive themselves. And yet, if a whole occupation is suddenly displaced, what do we do? We just came through an election where the loss of jobs was a big topic. Maybe truck drivers don't want to be trained to go on a computer. So, what are we going to do for the future? This is just another challenge that we face as technology advances. And that's why we're here today.

So, thanks. I'm looking forward to it.

Senator CRUZ. Thank you, Senator Nelson.

I'd now like to introduce our witnesses.

The first witness is Dr. Eric Horvitz, who is the interim Co-Chair of the Partnership on Artificial Intelligence and serves as the Managing Director of the Microsoft Research Redmond Lab. Dr. Horvitz's research contributions span theoretical and practical challenges with computing systems that learn from data and that can perceive, reason, and decide. His efforts have helped to bring multiple systems and services into the world, including innovations in transportation, healthcare, aerospace, e-commerce, online services, and operating systems.

Dr. Andrew Moore is the Dean of the School of Computer Science at Carnegie Mellon University. Dr. Moore's background is in statistical machine learning, artificial intelligence, robotics, and statistical computation of large volumes of data, including decision and control algorithms.

Mr. Greg Brockman is the Cofounder and Chief Technology Officer of OpenAI, a nonprofit artificial intelligence research company. Prior to OpenAI, Mr. Brockman was the CTO of Stripe, a financial technology company that builds tools enabling Web commerce.

And Dr. Steve Chien is the Technical Group Supervisor of the Artificial Intelligence Group and the Senior Research Scientist in the Mission Planning and Execution Section at NASA's Jet Propulsion Laboratory.

I would also note that Dr. Andrew Futreal was set to testify at our hearing today, but, unfortunately, due to weather issues, he was unable to travel to D.C. today. Dr. Futreal is the Chair of the Department of Genomic Medicine at The University of Texas MD Anderson Cancer Center, in my hometown of Houston. We thank him for his previously submitted written testimony. And if there are no objections, I would like to submit Dr. Futreal's testimony into the hearing record.

[The prepared statement of Dr. Futreal follows:]

PREPARED STATEMENT OF DR. ANDY FUTREAL, CHAIR, DEPARTMENT OF GENOMIC MEDICINE, THE UNIVERSITY OF TEXAS MD ANDERSON CANCER CENTER

Subcommittee Chairman Cruz, Ranking Member Peters, and members of this committee, thank you all very much for the opportunity to testify before you today. My name is Andy Futreal and I am Chair of the Department of Genomic Medicine at The University of Texas MD Anderson Cancer Center.

We are now entered into a completely unprecedented time in the history of medicine. We have the ability to investigate the fundamental molecular underpinnings of disease, to leverage technology and computational capabilities with the real prospect of fundamentally altering the natural history of disease. We can now determine each individual's genetic blueprint with relative speed and accuracy at a cost of less than a millionth of the price tag of the first human genome sequenced just a little more than 13 years ago. We are moving into an era of tackling the sequencing of very large groups of individuals and defining the role of common variation, that which is shared by more than 1–5 percent of the population, in health, risk and disease. The challenge of reducing this watershed of data into practical implementation to improve human health and provide better care for patients is upon us. The opportunities to improve and tailor healthcare delivery—the right drug for the right patient at the right time with the right follow-up—are being driven by exploiting computational approaches and so-called "big data". AI and machine learning approaches have the potential to help drive insights and deliver improved standards of care. Taking oncology as the proving ground where a very great deal of these efforts are currently focused, there are several challenges, opportunities and issues that present themselves.

The clinically meaningful implementation of machine-assisted learning and AI is, of course, crucially dependent on data—lots of it. Herein lies perhaps the biggest challenge. Substantial and varied clinical data is generated on every patient cared for every day. These data are generally held in non-interoperable systems whose principle purpose is to facilitate tracking of activities/services/tests for billing purposes. The richest clinical data is effectively locked in various dictated and transcribed notes detailing patients' clinical course, responses, problems and outcomes from the various treatments/interventions undertaken. We need to further develop capabilities to both get these data from their source systems and standardize their ongoing collection as practically as possible.

As well, a proportion of those under our care take part in research studies, generating research data in both the clinical and more translational/basic science realms. These data, including increasing amounts of detailed large-scale genomic sequencing information, are not generally available for integration with clinical data on a per-patient or aggregate basis in a way that would facilitate implementation of advanced analytics. The ability to purposefully integrate clinical and research data for analytics, without the need for predetermining and rigidly standardizing all data inputs up front is what is needed.

There are substantial opportunities for AI, again anchoring in oncology by way of example. Perhaps the most concise way of framing where we need to be headed, in my view, is the concept of real-time "patients like mine" analytics. Leveraging clinical, molecular, exposure and lifestyle data of patients that have been treated before to understand and predict what the best choices are for the current patient. But even more so, not just choice of therapeutic but how to improve and intercede as needed in management such that positive outcome chances are maximized. We need to make predictive analytics the norm, learning from every patient to improve the outcome of the next. Importantly, we need to be thinking now about training our best and brightest in the next generation of physicians and medical professionals to drive this progress, as it will take a new wave of computationally savvy individuals to build, train and grow these systems. Further, we need to think carefully about how we promote data sharing, particularly in the clinical arena. Open access is a laudable goal, but one that must be tempered with the relevant privacy and security practices. Facilitated collaboration on specific topics with honest broker mechanisms to demonstrate rapid progress and real value in data sharing early will, I think, be key.

At MD Anderson, we have been exploring the possible utilities of AI and related technologies in collaboration with IBM. We are utilizing the Watson platform for cognitive computing to train an expert system for patient-centric treatment recommendation and management. Currently, we are evaluating performance in the context of lung cancer. Future work reflects the challenges and opportunities that the entire field faces—namely that of what to deploy in the near-term where dissemination of expert knowledge in the context of rule-based approaches could have significant impact on potentially improving standard of care and where to take efforts in the longer term with learning, AI type approaches.

The ability to have data-driven, AI empowered point-of-care analytics holds the promise of improving the standard of care in medically underserved areas, of guaranteeing that every patient—regardless of zip code—can be assured of up-to-date and appropriate care taking into account their own particular data and circumstance. A massive undertaking to be sure, but one that is, I believe, within our collective grasp.

I thank you again for the opportunity to testify before this committee and I would be happy to answer any questions you may have.

Senator CRUZ. With that, we will move to the testimony, although I will note for each of you that your experience and wisdom in this topic will be welcomed and sorely needed, and intelligence, artificial or otherwise, is not something we deal with often, because this is the United States Congress.

[Laughter.]

Senator CRUZ. And with that, Dr. Horvitz, you may give your testimony.

STATEMENT OF ERIC HORVITZ, TECHNICAL FELLOW AND DIRECTOR, MICROSOFT RESEARCH—REDMOND LAB, MICROSOFT CORPORATION; INTERIM CO-CHAIR, PARTNERSHIP ON ARTIFICIAL INTELLIGENCE

Dr. HORVITZ. Thank you, Chairman Cruz, Ranking Member Peters, and members of the Subcommittee. And good afternoon. And thank you for hosting this discussion on AI. It's fabulous.

To start, AI is not one thing. AI is a constellation of disciplines, including computer vision, machine learning, language understanding, reasoning and planning, and robotics, but they're all aimed at a shared aspiration, the scientific understanding of thought and intelligent behavior, and in developing computing systems based on these understandings.

Many advances over the 60-year history of AI have now—are now actually part of our daily lives. Just consider the AI route-planning algorithms we use daily in our GPS systems. And, while we've seen many advances over time, it's clear that we're now at an inflection point. We're seeing an acceleration of AI competencies in many areas. And the inflection is driven by a confluence of several factors. And these include the unprecedented quantities of data that have come available with the widespread digitization of our lives, increases in computing power over time, and the recent jumps in the prowess of our algorithms, the methods we use, particularly machine-learning methods that learn to predict and to diagnose from data.

The advances are putting unprecedented technologies in the hands of people, including real-time speech-to-speech translation among languages now available from Microsoft's Skype services, and computer vision for assisting drivers. AI technology that is already available today could save thousands of lives and many billions of dollars if properly translated into practice. And these key— and the key opportunities before us include healthcare, transportation, education, as well as agriculture, manufacturing, and increasing accessibility for those with special needs. Other directions that are critical include using AI advances to enhance the resilience and capacity of critical infrastructure, like our electrical power grid and road network.

So, let's take as an example healthcare, to start. It's—AI is a veritable sleeping giant for healthcare. AI technologies will be extremely valuable for handling acute as well as chronic illnesses and for making our hospitals safer. As an example, we've built systems that can predict patient outcomes and that make patient-specific recommendations to allocate scarce resources. And these prototypes have been applied to address such challenges as chronic diseases, hospital readmissions, hospital-associated infections, and catching preventable errors in hospitals responsible for over a quarter of a million deaths per year in the United States.

And, while on the topic of saving lives, advances in pattern-recognition systems enable us to develop effective automated braking and control systems that will keep us safer. We could take a big cut out of those 30,000 deaths that we've become accustomed to tolerating every year in our country. And we don't often think about the 300,000 incapacitating injuries on our roads every year.

Numerous other AI innovations can help with safe driving. This week, we just published—our team just published results that show how we can leverage data from Minneapolis to build a routing system that identifies the safest routes to take, considering a multitude of factors at any moment, even how the sun is shining and the glare that it produces.

Moving forward, key research directions in AI include focusing on human-AI collaboration, ensuring the robustness, safety, and security of AI systems, and identifying and addressing the ethical, legal, economic, and broader societal influences of AI.

As an example of important research, we need to endow systems with the ability to explain their reasoning to people. People need to trust systems to use them effectively. And such trust requires transparency. There's also important work to be done with developing robust and resilient AI systems, especially when these systems are used for high stakes, safety-critical applications amidst the complexities of the open world.

We must also be aware that AI systems can present new kinds of attack surfaces that can be disrupted by cyberattacks, so it's important to address rising cyber vulnerabilities as we develop and field these more capable AI systems.

Another area of importance is the influence of AI on our Nation's workforce and economy. And, while estimates vary, the economic influence of AI will likely be in multiples of trillions of dollars. However, along with the expected benefits come concerns with how AI will affect jobs and income disparities. And these are important issues. We must closely reflect, monitor, and plan to ensure a smooth transition to a world where AI plays a more important role.

One thing for sure is that we urgently need to prioritize the training and retraining of the U.S. workforce so that our workforce skills are aligned with needs. We also need to double down on investments in STEM education and training. And, moving forward, continued strong and public and private sector support of research and studies on the scientific and socioeconomic challenges of AI will be critical to ensuring that people in society get the most out of AI advances.

So, in summary, we expect AI advances to raise our quality of life, to empower citizens in new ways. But, with—as with any technical advance, we need to invest efforts to study and address potential challenges, concerns, inequities that may come along with the benefits that we expect from AI.

Thanks very much.

[The prepared statement of Dr. Horvitz follows:]

PREPARED STATEMENT OF ERIC HORVITZ, TECHNICAL FELLOW AND DIRECTOR, MICROSOFT RESEARCH—REDMOND LAB, MICROSOFT CORPORATION

"REFLECTIONS ON THE STATUS AND FUTURE OF ARTIFICIAL INTELLIGENCE"

Chairman Cruz, Ranking Member Peters, and Members of the Subcommittee, my name is Eric Horvitz, and I am a Technical Fellow and Director of Microsoft's Research Lab in Redmond, Washington. While I am also serving as Co-Chair of a new organization, the Partnership on Artificial Intelligence, I am speaking today in my role at Microsoft.

We appreciate being asked to testify about AI and are committed to working collaboratively with you and other policymakers so that the potential of AI to benefit our country, and to people and society more broadly can be fully realized.

With my testimony, I will first offer a historical perspective of AI, a definition of AI and discuss the inflection point the discipline is currently facing. Second, I will highlight key opportunities using examples in the healthcare and transportation industries. Third, I will identify the important research direction many are taking with AI. Next, I will attempt to identify some of the challenges related to AI and offer my thoughts on how best to address them. Finally, I will offer several recommendations.

What is Artificial Intelligence?

Artificial intelligence (AI) refers to a set of computer science disciplines aimed at the scientific understanding of the mechanisms underlying thought and intelligent behavior and the embodiment of these principles in machines that can deliver value to people and society.

A simple definition of AI, drawn from a 1955 proposal that kicked off the modern field of AI, is pursuing how "to solve the kinds of problems now reserved for humans."[1] The authors of the founding proposal on AI also mentioned, "We think that a significant advance can be made in one or more of these problems if a carefully selected group of scientists work on it together for a summer." While progress has not proceeded as swiftly as the optimistic founders of the field may have expected, there have been ongoing advances over the decades from the sub-disciplines of AI, including *machine vision, machine learning, natural language understanding, reasoning and planning,* and *robotics.*

Highly visible AI achievements, such as DeepBlue's win over the world chess champion, have captured the imagination of the public. Such high-profile achievements have relayed a sense that the field is characterized by large jumps in capabilities. In reality, research and development (R&D) in the AI sub-disciplines have produced an ongoing stream of innovations. Numerous advances have become part of daily life, such as the widespread use of AI route-planning algorithms in navigation systems.[2] Many applications of AI execute "under the hood", including methods that perform machine learning and planning to enhance the functioning of computer operating systems or to better retrieve and rank search results. In some cases, AI systems have introduced breakthrough efficiencies without public recognition or fanfare. For example, in the mid- to late-1990s leading-edge machine vision methods for handwriting recognition were pressed into service by the U.S. Postal Service to recognize and route handwritten addresses on letters automatically.[3] High-speed variants of the first machines now sort through more than 25 billion letters per year, with estimated accrued savings of hundreds of millions of dollars.

AI at an Inflection Point

Over the last decade, there has been a promising inflection in the rate of development and fielding of AI applications. The acceleration has been driven by a confluence of several factors. A key influence behind the inflection is the availability of unprecedented streams of data, coupled with drops in the cost of storing and retrieving that data. Large quantities of structured and unstructured databases about human activities and content have become available via the digitization and the shift to the web of activities around commerce, science, communications, governance, education, and art and entertainment.

Other contributing factors include dramatic increases in available computing power, and jumps in the prowess of methods for performing machine learning and reasoning. There has been great activity in the machine learning area over the last thirty years with the development of a tapestry of algorithms for transforming data into components that can recognize patterns, perform diagnoses, and make predictions about future outcomes. The past thirty years of AI research also saw the rise and maturation of methods for representing and reasoning under uncertainty. Such methods jointly represent and manipulate both logical and probabilistic infor-

---

[1] McCarthy, J., Minsky, M.L., Rochester, N., Shannon, C.E. *A Proposal for the Dartmouth Summer Project on Artificial Intelligence,* Dartmouth University, May 1955.

[2] Hart, P.E., Nilsson, N.J., Raphael, B. A Formal Basis for the Heuristic Determination of Minimum Cost Paths. IEEE Transactions on Systems Science and Cybernetics Vol. SSC–4, No. 2, July 1968.

[3] Kim, G and Govindaraju, V., Handwritten Word Recognition for Real-Time Applications, Proceedings of the Third International Conference on Document Analysis and Recognition, August 1995.

mation. These methods draw from and extend methods that had been initially studied and refined in the fields of statistics, operations research, and decision science. Such methods for *learning and reasoning under uncertainty* have been critical for building and fielding AI systems that can grapple effectively with the inescapable incompleteness when immersed in real-world situations.

Over the last decade, there has been a renaissance in the use of a family of methods for machine learning known as *neural networks.*[4] A class of these algorithms referred to as *deep neural networks* are now being harnessed to significantly raise the quality and accuracy of such services as automatic speech recognition, face and object recognition from images and video, and natural language understanding. The methods are also being used to develop new computational capabilities for end users, such as real-time speech-to-speech translation among languages (*e.g.,* now available in Microsoft's Skype) and computer vision for assisting drivers with the piloting of cars (now fielded in the Tesla's models S and X).

Key Opportunities

AI applications explored to date frame opportunities ahead for leveraging current and forthcoming AI technologies. Pressing AI methods that are currently available into service could introduce new efficiencies into workflows and processes, help people with understanding and leveraging the explosion of data in scientific discovery and engineering, as well as assist people with solving a constellation of challenging real-world problems.[5]

Numerous commercial and societal opportunities can be addressed by using available data to build predictive models and then using the predictive models to help guide decisions. Such *data to predictions to decisions* pipelines can deliver great value and help build insights for a broad array of problems.[6] Key opportunities include AI applications in healthcare and biomedicine, accessibility, transportation, education, manufacturing, agriculture, and for increasing the effectiveness and robustness of critical infrastructure such as our electrical power grid.

Healthcare and transportation serve as two compelling examples where AI methods can have significant influence in the short-and longer-term.

Healthcare. AI can be viewed as a sleeping giant for healthcare. New efficiencies and quality of care can be obtained by leveraging a coupling of predictive models, decision analysis, and optimization efforts to support decisions and programs in healthcare. Applications span the handling of acute illnesses, longer-term disease management, and the promotion of health and preventative care. AI methods show promise for multiple roles in healthcare, including inferring and alerting about hidden risks of potential adverse outcomes, selectively guiding attention, care, and interventional programs where it is most needed, and reducing errors in hospitals.

On-site machine learning and decision support hinging on inference with predictive models can be used to identify and address potentially costly outcomes. Let's consider the challenge of reducing readmission rates. A 2009 study of Medicare-reimbursed patients who were hospitalized in 2004 found that approximately 20 percent of these patients were re-hospitalized within 30 days of their discharge from hospitals and that 35 percent of the patients were re-hospitalized within 90 days.[7] Beyond the implications of such readmissions for health, such re-hospitalizations were estimated to cost the Nation $17.4 billion in 2004. Studies have demonstrated that predictive models, learned from large-scale hospital datasets, can be used to identify patients who are at high risk of being re-hospitalized within a short time

---

[4] Neural network algorithms are descendants of statistical learning procedures developed in the 1950s, referred to as *perceptrons.* With neural networks, representations of patterns seen in training data are stored in a set of layers of large numbers of interconnected variables, often referred to as "neurons". The methods are inspired loosely (and in a very high-level manner) by general findings about the layering of neurons in vertebrate brains. Seven years ago, a class of neural networks, referred to as *deep neural networks,* developed decades earlier, were shown to provide surprising accuracies for pattern recognition tasks when trained with sufficient quantities of data.

[5] Multiple AI applications in support of people and society are presented here: E. Horvitz, *AI in Support of People and Society,* White House OSTP CCC AAAI meeting on AI and Social Good, Washington, D.C., June 2016. *(access video presentation)*

[6] E. Horvitz. *From Data to Predictions and Decisions: Enabling Evidence-Based Healthcare,* Data Analytic Series, Computing Community Consortium, Computing Research Association (CRA), September 2010.

[7] Coleman, E. Jencks, S., Williams, M. *Rehospitalizations among Patient in the Medicare Fee-for-Service Program,* The New England Journal of Medicine, 380:1418–1428, April 2009.

after they are discharged—and that such methods could be used to guide the allocation of special programs aimed at reducing readmission.[8]

AI methods can also play a major role in reducing costs and enhancing the quality of care for the difficult and ongoing challenge of managing chronic disorders. For example, congestive heart failure (CHF) is prevalent and expensive. The illness affects nearly 10 percent of people over 65 years. Medical costs and hospitalizations for CHF are estimated to be $35 billion per year in the U.S. CHF patients may hover at the edge of physiological stability and numerous factors can cause patients to spiral down requiring immediate hospitalization. AI methods trained with data can be useful to predict in advance potential challenges ahead and to allocate resources to patient education, sensing, and to proactive interventions that keep patients out of the hospital.

Machine learning, reasoning, and planning offer great promise for addressing the difficult challenge of keeping hospitals safe and efficient. One example is addressing the challenge with hospital-associated infections.[9] It is estimated that such infections affect 10 percent of people who are hospitalized and that they are a substantial contributor to death in the U.S. Hospital-associated infections have been linked to significant increases in hospitalization time and additional costs of tens of thousands of dollars per patient, and to nearly $7 billion of additional costs annually in the U.S. The CDC has been estimated that 90 percent of deaths due to hospital-associated infections can be prevented. A key direction is the application of predictive models and decision analyses to estimate patients' risk of illness and to guide surveillance and other preventative actions.

AI methods promise to complement the skills of physicians and create new forms of cognitive "safety nets" to ensure the effective care of hospitalized patients.[10] An Institute of Medicine (IOM) study in 2000 called attention to the problem of preventable errors in hospitals.[11] The study found that nearly 100,000 patients die in hospitals because of preventable human errors. The IOM estimate has been revised upward by several more recent studies. Studies in October 2013 and in May 2016 estimated that preventable errors in hospitals are the third leading cause of death in the U.S., only trailing behind heart disease and cancer. The two studies estimated deaths based in preventable error as exceeding 400,000 and 250,000 patients per year, respectively.[12,13] AI systems for catching errors via reminding and recognizing anomalies in best clinical practices could put a significant dent in the loss of nearly 1,000 citizens per day, and could save tens of thousands of patients per year.

The broad opportunities with the complementarity of AI systems and physicians could be employed in myriad ways in healthcare. For example, recent work in robotic surgery has explored how a robotic surgeon's assistant can work hand-in-hand to collaborate on complex surgical tasks. Other work has demonstrated how coupling machine vision for reviewing histological slides with human pathologists can significantly increase the accuracy of detecting cancer metastases.

Transportation. AI methods have been used widely in online services and applications for helping people with predictions about traffic flows with doing traffic-sensitive routing. Moving forward, AI methods can be harnessed in multiple ways to make driving safer and to expand the effective capacity of our existing roadway infrastructure. Automated cars enabled by advances in perception and robotics promise to enhance both flows on roads and to enhance safety. Longer-range possibilities include the fielding of large-scale automated public *microtransit* solutions on a city-wide basis. Such solutions could transform mobility within cities and could influence the overall structure and layout of cities over the longer-term.

Smart, automated driver alerting and assistance systems for collision avoidance show promise for saving hundreds of thousands of lives worldwide. Motor vehicle

---

[8] Bayati, M., Braverman, M., Gillam, M. Mack, K.M., Ruiz, G., Smith, M.S., Horvitz, E. *Data-Driven Decisions for Reducing Readmissions for Heart Failure: General Methodology and Case Study.* PLOS One Medicine. October 2014.

[9] Wiens, J., Guttag, J., and Horvitz, E., *Patient Risk Stratification with Time-Varying Parameters: A Multitask Learning Approach.* Journal of Machine Learning Research (JMLR), April 2016.

[10] Hauskrecht, M., Batal, I., Valko, M., Visweswaran, S., Cooper, G.F., Clermont, G., *Outlier Detection for Patient Monitoring and Alerting,* Journal of Biomedical Informatics, Volume 46, Issue 1, February 2013, Pages 47–55.

[11] *To Err Is Human: Building a Safer Health System,* Institute of Medicine: Shaping the Future, November 1999.

[12] James, John T. *A New, Evidence-based Estimate of Patient Harms Associated with Hospital Care,* Journal of Patient Safety, September 2013.

[13] Daniel, M., Makary, M. *Medical Error—The Third Leading Cause of Death in the U.S.,* BMJ, 353, 2016.

accidents are believed to be responsible for 1.2 million deaths and 20–50 million non-fatal injuries per year each year. NHTSA's Fatality Analysis Reporting System (FARS) shows that deaths in the U.S. due to motor vehicle injuries have been hovering at rates over 30,000 fatalities per year. In addition to deaths, it is important to include a consideration of the severe injuries linked to transportation. It is estimated that 300,000 to 400,000 people suffer incapacitating injuries every year in motor vehicles; in addition to the nearly 100 deaths per day, nearly one thousand Americans are being incapacitated by motor vehicle injuries every day.

Core errors based in the distraction of drivers and problems with control lead to road departures and read-end collisions. These expected problems with human drivers could be addressed with machine perception, smart alerting, and autonomous and semi-autonomous controls and compensation. AI methods that deliver inferences with low false-positive and false-negative rates for guiding braking and control could be pressed into service to save many thousands of lives and to avoid hundreds of thousands of life-changing injuries. Studies have found that a great proportion of motor vehicle accidents are caused by distraction and that nearly 20 percent of automobile accidents are believed to be failures to stop. Researchers have estimated that the use of smart warning, assisted braking, and autonomous braking systems could reduce serious injuries associated with rear-end collisions by nearly 50 percent.[14]

Myriad of opportunities. Healthcare and transportation are only two of the many sectors where AI technologies offer exciting advances. For example, machine learning, planning, and decision making can be harnessed to understand, strengthen, monitor, and extend such critical infrastructure such as our electrical power grid, roads, and bridges. In this realm, AI advances could help to address challenges and directions specified in the Energy Independence and Security Act of 2007 on the efficiency, resilience, and security of the U.S. power grid. In particular, there is opportunity to harness predictive models for predicting the load and availability of electrical power over time. Such predictions can lead to more effective plans for power distribution. Probabilistic troubleshooting methodologies can jointly harness knowledge of physical models and streams of data to develop models that could serve in proactive and real-time diagnoses of bottlenecks and failures, with a goal of performing interventions that minimize disruptions.

In another critical sector, AI methods can play an important role in the vitality and effectiveness of education and in continuing-education programs that we offer to citizens. As an example, data-centric analyses have been employed to develop predictive models for student engagement, comprehension, and frustration. Such models can be used in planners that create and update personalized education strategies.[15,16] Such plans could address conceptual bottlenecks and work to motivate and enhance learning. Automated systems could help teachers triage and troubleshoot rising challenges with motivation/engagement and help design ideal mixes of online and human-touch pedagogy.

Key Research Directions

R&D on AI continues to be exciting and fruitful with many directions and possibilities. Several important research directions include the following:

Supporting Human-AI collaboration. There is great promise for developing AI systems that complement and extend human abilities [17]. Such work includes developing AI systems that are human-aware and that can understand and augment human cognition. Research in this realm includes the development of systems that can recognize and understand the problems that people seek to solve, understanding human plans and intentions, and to recognize and address the cognitive blind spots and biases of people.[18] The latter opportunity can leverage rich results uncovered in over a century of work in cognitive psychology.

[14] Kusano, K.D. and Gabler, H.C., *Safety Benefits of Forward Collision Warning, Brake Assist, and Autonomous Braking Systems in Rear-End Collisions,* IEEE Transactions on Intelligent Transportation Systems, pages 1546–1555. Volume: 13(4), December 2012.

[15] K. Koedinger, S. D'Mello., E. McLauglin, Z. Pardos, C. Rose. *Data Mining and Education,* Wiley Interdisciplinary Reviews: Cognitive Science, 6(4): 333–353, July 2015.

[16] Rollinson, J. and Brunskill, E., *From Predictive Models to Instructional Policies,* International Educational Data Mining Society, International Conference on Educational Data Mining (EDM) Madrid, Spain, June 26–29, 2015.

[17] Licklider, J. C. R., *"Man-Computer Symbiosis",* IRE Transactions on Human Factors in Electronics, vol. HFE–1, 4–11, March 1960.

[18] Presentation: Horvitz, E., *Connections,* Sustained Achievement Award Lecture, ACM International Conference on Multimodal Interaction (ICMI), Seattle, WA, November 2015.

[19] E. Horvitz. *Principles of Mixed-Initiative User Interfaces.* Proceedings of CHI '99, ACM SIGCHI Conference on Human Factors in Computing Systems, Pittsburgh, PA, May 1999.

Research on human-AI collaboration also includes efforts on the coordination of a mix of initiatives by people and AI systems in solving problems. In such mixed-initiative systems, machines and people take turns at making contributions to solving a problem.[19,20] Advances in this realm can lead to methods that support humans and machines working together in a seamless, fluid manner.

Recent results have demonstrated that AI systems can learn about and extend peoples' abilities.[21] Research includes studies and methods that endow systems with an understanding about such important subtleties as the cost of an AI system interrupting people in different contexts with potentially valuable information or other contribution[22] and on predicting information that people will forget something that they need to remember in the context at hand.[23]

Causal discovery. Much of machine learning has focused on learning associations rather than causality. Causal knowledge is a critical aspect of scientific discovery and engineering. A longstanding challenge in the AI sub-discipline of machine learning has been identifying causality in an automated manner. There has been progress in this realm over the last twenty years. However, there is much to be done on developing tools to help scientists find rich causal models from large-scale sets of data.[24]

Unsupervised learning. Most machine learning is referred to as *supervised* learning. With supervised learning, data is directly or indirectly tagged by people who provide a learning system with specific labels, such as the goals or intentions of people, or health outcomes. There is deep interest and opportunity ahead with developing *unsupervised learning* methods that can learn without human-authored labels. We are all familiar with the apparent power that toddlers have with learning about the world without obvious detailed tagging or labeling. There is hope that we may one day better understand these kinds of abilities with the goal of harnessing them in our computing systems to learn more efficiently and with less reliance on people.

Learning physical actions in the open world. Research efforts have been underway on the challenges of enabling systems to do active exploration in simulated and real worlds that are aimed at endowing the systems with the ability to make predictions and to perform physical actions successfully. Such work typically involves the creation of training methodologies that enable a system to explore on its own, to perform multiple trials at tasks, and to learn from these experiences. Some of this work leverages methods in AI called *reinforcement learning,* where learning occurs via sets of experiences about the best actions or sequences of actions to take in different settings. Efforts to date include automatically training systems to recognize objects and to learn the best ways to grasp objects.[25]

Integrative intelligence. Many R&D efforts have focused on developing specific competencies in intelligence, such as systems capable of recognizing objects in images, understanding natural language, recognizing speech, and providing decision support in specific healthcare areas to assist pathologists with challenges in histopathology. There is a great opportunity to weave together multiple competencies such as vision and natural language to create new capabilities. For example, natural language and vision have been brought together in systems that can perform automated image captioning.[26,27] Other examples of integrative intelligence involve bringing together speech recognition, natural language understanding, vision, and sets of predictive models to support such challenges as constructing a sup-

[18] Presentation: Horvitz, E., *Connections,* Sustained Achievement Award Lecture, ACM International Conference on Multimodal Interaction (ICMI), Seattle, WA, November 2015.

[19] E. Horvitz. *Principles of Mixed-Initiative User Interfaces.* Proceedings of CHI '99, ACM SIGCHI Conference on Human Factors in Computing Systems, Pittsburgh, PA, May 1999.

[20] E. Horvitz. *Reflections on Challenges and Promises of Mixed-Initiative Interaction,* AAAI *Magazine* 28, Special Issue on Mixed-Initiative Assistants (2007).

[21] E. Kamar, S. Hacker, E. Horvitz. *Combining Human and Machine Intelligence in Large-scale Crowdsourcing, AAMAS 2012,* Valencia, Spain, June 2012.

[22] E. Horvitz and J. Apacible. *Learning and Reasoning about Interruption. Proceedings of the Fifth ACM International Conference on Multimodal Interfaces,* November 2003, Vancouver, BC, Canada.

[23] E. Kamar and E. Horvitz, *Jogger: Investigation of Principles of Context-Sensitive Reminding, Proceedings of International Conference on Autonomous Agents and Multiagent Systems (AAMAS 2011),* Tapei, May 2011.

[24] See efforts at the NIH BD2K Center for Causal Discovery: *http://www.ccd.pitt.edu/about/*

[25] J. Oberlin, S. Tellex. *Learning to Pick Up Objects Through Active Exploration, IEEE, August 2015.*

[26] H. Fang, S. Gupta, F. Iandola, R. Srivastava, L. Deng, P. Dollár, J. Gao, X. He, M. Mitchell, J. Platt, C. Zitnick, G. Zweig, *From Captions to Visual Concepts and Back,* CVPR 2015.

[27] Vinyals, O., Toshev, A., Bengio S. Dumitru, E., *Show and Tell: A Neural Image Caption*

portive automated administrative assistant.[28] There is much opportunity ahead in efforts in integrative intelligence that seek to weave together multiple AI competencies into greater wholes that can perform rich tasks.

Advances in platform and systems. Specific needs for advances with data-center scale systems and innovative hardware have come to the fore to support the training and execution of large-scale neural network models. New research at the intersection of learning and reasoning algorithms, computing hardware, and systems software will likely be beneficial in supporting AI innovations. Such research is being fielded in platforms that are becoming available from large companies in the technology sector.

Development tools and "democratization of AI". New types of development tools and platforms can greatly assist with development, debugging, and fielding of AI applications. R&D is ongoing at large IT companies on providing developers with cloud-based programmatic interfaces (*e.g.,* Microsoft's Cognitive Services) and client-based components for performing valuable inference tasks (*e.g.,* detect emotion in images). Also, learning toolkits are being developed that enable researchers and engineers to do machine learning investigations and to field classifiers (*e.g.,* Microsoft's CNTK and Google's TensorFlow). Other development environments are being developed for creating integrative AI solutions that can be used by engineers to assemble systems that rely on the integration of multiple competencies (natural language understanding, speech recognition, vision, reasoning about intentions of people, etc.) that must work together in a tightly coordinated manner in real-time applications.

Challenges

Economics and jobs. Over the last several years, the AI competencies with seeing, hearing, and understanding language have grown significantly. These growing abilities will lead to the fielding of more sophisticated applications that can address tasks that people have traditionally performed. Thus, AI systems will likely have significant influences on jobs and the economy. Few dispute the assertion that AI advances will increase production efficiencies and create new wealth. McKinsey & Company has estimated that advanced digital capabilities could add 2.2 trillion U.S. dollars to the U.S. GDP by 2025. There are rising questions about how the fruits of AI productivity will distributed and on the influence of AI on jobs. Increases in the competencies of AI systems in both the cognitive and physical realms will have influences on the distribution, availability, attraction, and salaries associated with different jobs. We need to focus attention on reflection, planning, and monitoring to address the potential disruptive influences of AI on jobs in the U.S.—and to work to understand the broad implications of new forms of automation provided by AI for domestic and international economics. Important directions for study include seeking an understanding of the needs and value of education and the geographic distribution of rising and falling job opportunities.

There is an urgent need for training and re-training of the U.S. workforce so as to be ready for expected shifts in workforce needs and in the shifts in distributions of jobs that are fulfilling and rewarding to workers. In an economy increasingly driven by advances in digital technology, increasing numbers of jobs are requiring a degree in one of the STEM (science, technology, engineering, and math) fields. There is growing demand for people with training in computer science, with estimates suggesting that by 2024, the number of computer and information analyst jobs will increase by almost 20 percent. For companies to thrive in the digital, cloud-driven economy, the skills of employees must keep pace with advances in technology. It has been estimated as many as 2 million jobs could go unfilled *in the U.S. manufacturing sector* during the next decade because of a shortage of people with the right technical skills.[29] Investing in education can help to prepare and adapt our workforce to what we expect will be a continuing shift in the distribution of jobs, and for the changing demands on human labor.

Beyond ensuring that people are trained to take on fulfilling, well-paid positions, providing STEM education and training to larger number of citizens will be critical for U.S. competitiveness. We are already facing deficits in our workforce: The Bureau of Labor Statistics estimates that there are currently over 5 million unfilled positions in the U.S. Many of those jobs are those created due to new technologies. This suggests that there are tremendous opportunities for people with the right

---

[28] D. Bohus and E. Horvitz. *Dialog in the Open World: Platform and Applications, ICMI–MLMI 2009: International Conference on Multimodal Interaction,* Cambridge, MA. November, 2009.

[29] The Manufacturing Institute and Deloitte, *"The skills gap in U.S. manufacturing: 2015 and beyond."*, 2015.

skills to help U.S. companies to create products and services that can, in turn, drive additional job creation and create further economic growth.

Shortages of people who have training in sets of skills that are becoming increasingly relevant and important could pose serious competitive issues for companies and such shortages threaten the long-term economic health of the U.S. Without addressing the gap in skills, we'll likely see a widening of the income gap between those who have the skills to succeed in the 21st century and those who do not. Failing to address this gap will leave many people facing an uncertain future—particularly women, young people, and those in rural and underserved communities. Working to close this divide will be an important step to addressing income inequality and is one of the most important actions we can take.

Safety and robustness in the open world. Efforts to employ AI systems in high-stakes, safety critical applications will become more common with the rising competency of AI technologies.[30] Such applications include automated and semi-automated cars and trucks, surgical assistants, automation of commercial air transport, and military operations and weapon systems, including uses in defensive and offensive systems. Work is underway on ensuring that systems in safety critical areas perform robustly and in accordance with human preferences. Efforts on safety and robustness will require careful, methodical studies that address the multiple ways that learning and reasoning systems may perform costly, unintended actions.[31] Costly outcomes can result from erroneous behaviors stemming from attacks on one or more components of AI systems by malevolent actors. Other concerns involve problems associated with actions that are not considered by the system. Fears have also been expressed that smart systems might be able to make modifications and to shift their own operating parameters and machinery. These classes of concern frame directions for R&D.

Efforts and directions on safety and robustness include the use of techniques in computer science referred to as *verification* that prove constraints on behaviors, based on offline analyses or on real-time monitoring. Other methods leverage and extend results developed in the realm of adaptive control, on robust monitoring and control of complex systems. Control-theoretic methods can be extended with models of sensor error and with machine learning about the environment to provide guarantees of safe operation, given that assumptions and learnings about the world hold.[32] Such methods can provide assurance of safe operation at a specified tolerated probability of failure. There are also opportunities for enhancing the robustness of AI systems by leveraging principles of *failsafe design* developed in other areas of engineering.[33] Research is also underway on methods for building systems that are robust to incompleteness in their models, and that can respond appropriately to *unknown* unknowns faced in the open world.[34] Beyond research, best practices may be needed on effective testing, structuring of trials, and reporting when fielding new technologies in the open world.

A related, important area for R&D on safety critical AI applications centers on the unique challenges that can arise in systems that are jointly controlled by people and machines. Opportunities include developing systems that explicitly consider human attention and intentions, that provide people with explanations of machine inferences and actions, and that work to ensure that people comprehend the state of problem solving—especially as control is passed between machines and human decision making. There is an opportunity to develop and share best practices on how systems signal and communicate with humans in settings of shared responsibility.

Ethics of autonomous decisions. Systems that make autonomous decisions in the world may have to make trades and deliberate about the costs and benefits of rich, multidimensional outcomes—under uncertainty. For example, it is feasible that an

---

[30] T.G. Dietterich and E.J. Horvitz, *Rise of Concerns about AI: Reflections and Directions.* Communications of the ACM, Vol. 58 No. 10, pages 38–40, October 2015.

[31] Amodei, D., Olah, C., Steinhardt, J., Christiano, P., Schulman, J., Mané, D., *Concrete Problems in AI Safety,* arXiv, 25 July 2016.

[32] D. Sadigh, A. Kapoor, *Safe Control Under Uncertainty with Probabiliistic Signal Temporal Logic,* Robotics: Science and Systems, RSS 2016.

[33] Overview presentation on safety and control of AI can be found here: E. Horvitz, *Reflections on Safety and Artificial Intelligence,* White House OSTP–CMU *Meeting on Safety and Control of AI,* June 2016. (*view video presentation*).

[34] One challenge that must be considered when fielding applications for safety critical tasks is with transfer of applications from the closed world of test scenarios to the open world of fielded technologies. Systems developed in the laboratory or in test facilities can be surprised by unexpected situations in the open world—a world that contains unmodeled situations, including sets of *unknown unknowns* stemming from incompleteness in a system's perceptions and understandings. Addressing incompleteness and unknown unknowns is an interesting AI research challenge.

automated driving system may have to reason about actions that differentially influence the likelihood that passengers versus pedestrians are injured. As systems become more competent and are granted greater autonomy in different areas, it is important that the values that guide their decisions are aligned with the values of people and with greater society. Research is underway on the representation, learning, transparency, and specification of values and tradeoffs in autonomous and semi-autonomous systems.

Fairness, bias, transparency. There is a growing community of researchers with interest in identifying and addressing potential problems with fairness and bias in AI systems.[35] Datasets and the classifications or predictions made by systems constructed from the data can be biased. Implicit biases in data and in systems can arise because of unmodeled or poorly understood limitations or constraints on the process of collection of data, the shifting of the validity of data as it ages, and using systems for inferences and decisions for populations or situations that differ greatly from the populations and situations that provided the training data As an example, predictive models have been used to assist with decision making in the realm of criminal justice. Models trained on datasets have been used to assist judges with decisions about bail and about the release of people charged with crimes in advance of their court dates. Such decisions can enhance the lives of people and reduce costs. However, great caution must be used with ensuring that datasets do not encode and amplify potential systematic biases in the way the data is defined and collected. Research on fairness, biases, and accountability and the performance of machine-learned models for different constituencies is critically important. The importance of this area will only grow in importance as AI methods are used with increasing frequency to advise decision makers about the best actions in high-stakes settings. Such work may lead to best practices on the collection, usage, and the sharing of datasets for testing, inspection, and experimentation. Transparency and openness may be especially important in applications in governance.

Manipulation. It is feasible that methods employing machine learning, planning, and optimization could be used to create systems that work to influence peoples' beliefs and behavior. Further, such systems could be designed to operate in manner that is undetectable by those being influenced. More work needs to be done to study, detect, and monitor such activity.

Privacy. With the rise of the centrality of data-centric analyses and predictive models come concerns about privacy. We need to consider the potential invasion in the privacy of individuals based on inferences that can be made from seemingly innocuous data. Other efforts on privacy include methods that allow data to be used for machine learning and reasoning yet maintains the privacy of individuals. Approaches include methods for anonymizing data via injecting noise[36], sharing only certain kinds of summarizing statistics, providing people with controls that enable them to trade off the sharing of data for enhanced personalization of services[37], and using different forms of encryption. There is much work to be done on providing controls and awareness to people about the data being shared and how it is being used to enhance services for themselves and for larger communities.

Cybersecurity. New kinds of automation can present new kinds of "attack surfaces" that provide opportunities for manipulation and disruption by cyberattacks by state and non-state actors. As mentioned above, it is critical to do extensive analyses of the new attack surfaces and the associated vulnerabilities that come with new applications of AI. New classes of attack are also feasible, including "machine learning attacks," involving the injection of erroneous or biased training data into datasets. Important directions include hardware and software-based security and encryption, new forms of health monitoring, and reliance on principles of failsafe design.

Recommendations

We recommend the following to catalyze innovation among our basic and applied AI communities across government, academia, industry, and non-profit sectors:

- Public-sector research investments are vital for catalyzing innovation on AI principles, applications, and tools. Such funding can leverage opportunities for collaborating and coordinating with industry and other sectors to help facilitate innovation.

---

[35] See Fairness, Accountability, and Transparency in Machine Learning (FATML) conference site: *http://www.fatml.org/*

[36] Differential privacy ref: Dwork, C.: Differential Privacy. In: Proceedings of the 33rd International Colloquium on Automata, Languages and Programming (ICALP) (2), pp. 1–12 (2006).

[37] A. Krause and E. Horvitz. *A Utility-theoretic Approach to Privacy in Online Services, Journal of Artificial Intelligence Research,* 39 (2010) 633–662.

- Research investments are needed at the intersection of AI, law, policy, psychology, and ethics to better understand and monitor the social and societal consequences of AI.
- Governments should create frameworks that enable citizens and researchers to have easy access to government curated datasets where appropriate, taking into consideration privacy and security concerns.
- With the goal of developing guidelines and best practices, governments, industry, and civil society should work together to weigh the range of ethical questions and issues that AI applications raise in different sectors. As experience with AI broadens, it may make sense to establish more formal industry standards that reflect consensus about ethical issues but that do not impede innovation and progress with AI and its application in support of people and society.
- In an era of increasing data collection and use, privacy protection is more important than ever. To foster advances in AI that benefit society, policy frameworks must protect privacy without limiting innovation. For example, governments should encourage the exploration and development of techniques that enable analysis of large datasets without revealing individual identities.
- We need to invest in training that prepares people for high-demand STEM jobs. Governments should also invest in high-quality worker retraining programs for basic skills and for certifications and ongoing education for those already in the workforce. A first step is to identify the skills that are most in demand. Governments can develop and deliver high-quality workforce retraining programs or provide incentives and financial resources for private and nonprofit organizations to do so.

Thank you for the opportunity to testify. I look forward to answering your questions.

Senator CRUZ. Thank you, Dr. Horvitz.
Dr. Moore.

STATEMENT OF DR. ANDREW W. MOORE, DEAN, SCHOOL OF COMPUTER SCIENCE, CARNEGIE MELLON UNIVERSITY

Dr. MOORE. Thank you, Chairman Cruz, Ranking Member Peters, and members of the Subcommittee, for convening this really important meeting.

What I want to do with this testimony is to offer three takeaways. First, what AI is and what it isn't right now. The "artificial" in artificial intelligence is there for a reason. Second, I will explain why things are changing so quickly right now. And third, I want to talk about the thing that keeps me awake at night regarding U.S. competitiveness in AI.

So, what is AI? When one of my students decides to build an AI, they always end up doing two things. One, they make sure the computer can perceive and understand the world through computer vision and through big data. Second, they do massive search, which means, in all these examples we've talked about, such as a car finding a route, the computer searches to find the best of billions, and sometimes quintillions, of possibilities, and does that very quickly and efficiently. And that's happening all the time. When you ask Siri a question, what's happening up there in the cloud is, it is essentially trying out about 10 billion possible answers to your question and searching over them to score each one as to how likely it is to make you satisfied. If an autonomous car is about to hit a deer, and it's about .2 of a second to impact, it can spend the first 20th of a second gaming out millions of possibilities of what it can do, what the deer is going to do, to maximize the chance that people are going to survive. So, that's what's going on in AI. It is perception through big data and search.

What has really changed in the last couple of years is, through the efforts of the United States in big data, we now have computers which can perceive enough of this to be useful. And this means that there's now a big land grab going on for researchers and entrepreneurs and students for finding all the places where we can use this. For example, this picture here is of Sebastien LePage, who is V.P. of Operations at Kinova, a robotics arm company, working with Carnegie Mellon faculty on the question of, if you are unable to use anything below your neck, but you want to indicate by nodding at something that you'd like to pick it up, perhaps nod again to say you want to bring it to your mouth, searching over the billions of possible things the arm can do safely to find the one which is most likely to make you, as the user, happy. This is an unambiguously good use of technology applicable to tens of thousands of our veterans, for example.

But, what excites me, and the reason I'm in this business right now, is that there are thousands of stories like this happening, and my students and faculty and folks all across the country who have the skills are exploring the ways of doing this.

For example, one of our undergraduate students, working by herself using open AI tools, managed to quickly come up with a system for checking open Internet records to detect sex traffickers. And her algorithm has saved, you know, a couple of hundred young women from sex trafficking. That's one person who had the skills able to do this.

Another example, this wasn't possible 12 months ago. Now we have drones zooming quickly through forests, able to dodge trees as they're going, because they can now afford to plan so fast to avoid trees in sub-second time. Many other examples, so many that I could keep us going for half an hour. They all just make me so excited.

But, the thing that keeps me awake at night on all of this is the talent war. I really, really beseech that, together, we can get a million of the current middle-school students in the country to become AI experts over the next 5 to 10 years. At the moment, we have a tiny fraction—I would say less than 1 percent—of the people available to work in this area who could work in this area. If you duplicated these four panel members a hundred times each, we still would have too much to do when it comes to taking advantage of all these opportunities.

I estimate that, when an Internet company hires one of our students, they're making 5 to 10 million dollars per student just by having that person on their payroll. And so, the bidding wars for these talents are huge. And our students, instead of necessarily moving to work on AI for the Veterans Administration or AI for helping protect our warfighter, the majority of them are simply going off to Internet companies, which is fine, but I want them in all the other sectors of our economy, as well.

Similarly, if you look at every one of the big advances in artificial intelligence that are now active, they came from university professors—the majority of them from U.S. university professors. We are beginning to lose many of our university professors to industry, and that is damaging our seed corn. Our university professors who are AI experts are looking for sustained, stable funding, not necessarily lots of funding, so that they can realize their dreams of doing things like this.

So, I'm very excited. I'm very grateful for this subcommittee for shining a light on this important issue. I think the future is bright, but it really is an AI race at the moment.

[The prepared statement of Dr. Moore follows:]

PREPARED STATEMENT OF DR. ANDREW W. MOORE, DEAN, SCHOOL OF COMPUTER SCIENCE, CARNEGIE MELLON UNIVERSITY

Thank you Chairman Cruz, Ranking Member Peters, and Members of the Subcommittee for convening this important hearing on Artificial Intelligence (AI). I am honored to be here and to be joined by colleagues who are advancing the science, technology, business models, critical applications, and policy considerations of AI in the service of the United States and humanity.

My name is Andrew Moore. I am the Dean of the School of Computer Science at Carnegie Mellon University and former Vice President at Google responsible for Machine Learning technology. I appreciate your leadership in focusing on the future of science, innovation, and American competitiveness and on the role that AI can play. The policies and strategies we adopt over the next several years will determine if the United States wins the race to lead this technological revolution as well as the resulting benefits for our citizens.

Introduction: Perspectives on the Future of AI from a Journey in Computer Science

Building upon fifty years of research, strategic Federal investments, dramatic advances in machine learning, and the explosion in available digital data, we no longer describe AI as a technology from the future: it is around us in our phones, our vehicles and in defense of our borders. AI tools are already making doctors better at diagnosing diseases and ensuring patients obtain the latest effective treatments.

AI-empowered personalized learning will enable teachers to better reach and engage every student. Powerful new AI cyber tools will provide a new and more definitive defense against a world increasingly populated by hackers intent on criminal or state-sponsored attacks on American institutions, businesses and citizens. Adaptive, learning robotic systems will enable small manufacturers to cost-effectively change product lines more rapidly—even realizing mass production economies from "quantity one" to compete with foreign firms utilizing cheap labor. The ability to combine autonomous vehicles with public transit will unlock urban congestion, transform land use, enhance safety, and enable cities to focus on the most critical human elements of mobility. And, the potential applications of AI as powerful tools in national defense and homeland security will make us safer, even in the face of growing threats. In each of these areas, powerful opportunities exist to eradicate the barriers of distance, economic isolation, and limited economic opportunities, as well as making us a smarter, more productive, healthier, safer nation.

Some economists assert that increased deployment of AI could represent a powerful economic stimulus for the nation—perhaps adding as much as 2 points to annual GDP growth by 2035.[1] There are also economists who warn that the advance of AI applications could exacerbate income inequality and threaten a wide number of middle income jobs.[2]

I am not an economist by training. I bring to this hearing perspectives shaped by my journey over three decades as a computer scientist and a technology business leader. As a university researcher I had the opportunity to develop machine learning capabilities that enable emergency room physicians to better predict the illnesses and patient levels they are likely to confront as weather and virus outbreak patterns evolve. This experience provided a window on how powerful AI applications can be to improve the delivery of vital services to those in need.

At Google I helped develop advanced machine learning platforms to more effectively connect consumers to information by making search engine algorithms smarter and more powerful. That experience also taught me how AI tools can democratize access to information and unleash the energy of entrepreneurs to capitalize on the power of these platforms to bring products to consumers in a way that would have never been possible before.

For example, enabling consumers to see the 200,000 new dresses that are produced each day in the world helps to unleash the creativity and entrepreneurship of dress makers and fashion designers in an unprecedented way, whether they are large companies or a small startup, in a major city or a rural community.

But, as this Committee knows well, we face far broader and more daunting and important challenges as a nation than matching consumers with dresses.

Now, as Dean of the #1 Computer Science School in the U.S., I have the wonderful opportunity to engage with a new generation of students—and their faculty mentors—who are drawn to computer science because they want to focus their careers on applying AI to tackle our biggest societal challenges. They arrive at this with the clear eyed recognition that, as has been true with all new innovation, they must also address the potential negative impacts these technologies may bring. These experiences make me very optimistic that we can harness the power of AI to grow our economy and improve our quality of life while also acting definitively to mitigate any potential disruptions this new technology, like any new technology, can bring. New technology will always come. We must contribute to its use for good.

My journey as a computer scientist leaves me certain that AI can create fundamentally new economic opportunities and be a powerful resource for addressing our most pressing challenges in areas of security, health care, better food production, and a new era of growth in manufacturing. At the same time, it can fundamentally transform the nature of work, as well as create new challenges in areas such as privacy. The key is a focused national strategy to nurture and attract the best talent, including applying new AI learning tools to aid workers in need of retraining; to enhance discovery and commercialization; and to create a business and regulatory environment that rewards innovation.

Carnegie Mellon and the AI Revolution

My perspective has been heavily shaped by the culture of discovery at the School of Computer Science at Carnegie Mellon. The development of Artificial Intelligence was launched 60 years ago at a seminal gathering at Dartmouth University in the summer of 1956. Two of the four scientists who led that session, Allen Newell and Herbert Simon, were CMU faculty and had already created the first AI program. Since that time, with strong support from Federal research agencies, our faculty have pursued disruptive innovations that have help fuel the development of AI. These innovations include multithreaded computing, speech and natural language understanding, computer vision, software engineering methodology, self-driving robotic platforms, distributed file systems and more.

Today well over 100 faculty and 1,000 students at Carnegie Mellon are engaged in AI-related research and education. In addition to advancing breakthroughs fundamental to the building blocks of AI systems, Carnegie Mellon faculty and student researchers have applied advances in AI to the early detection of disease outbreaks, combating sex trafficking rings, detection of emerging terror threats in social media, and to the development of cognitive tutoring tools that are now deployed in middle schools, high schools, and colleges in every state in the Nation. CMU alumni and faculty (typically on leave) hold leading positions in each of the major companies driving AI development, including at Microsoft, IBM, Google, Amazon, and Apple. CMU spin-off companies have been a catalyst to advancing AI innovations.

Fundamental Building Blocks of AI Systems

AI is defined as "the scientific understanding of the mechanisms underlying thought and intelligent behavior and their embodiment in machines."[3] As we strategize on the next AI steps at Carnegie Mellon University, it helps us to break AI research into two broad categories: Autonomous AIs and Cognitive Assistant AIs. An Autonomous System has to make low level decisions by itself, for example a car that only has half a second to react to a collision simply cannot wait for a human. Or a constellation of satellites that has lost communications with the ground needs to figure out what they should be observing and transmitting to the ground while trading off the need to protect their advanced sensors against an energy attack. Cognitive Assistants, on the other hand, work hand in hand with a human: our smart phones telling us how to get to our kid's dental appointments are a simple example. Much more advanced examples include CMU faculty Sidd Srinivasa's work on intelligent robot arms controlled by humans in wheelchairs with high spinal cord injuries.

AI involves transforming raw data—often massive amounts of raw data—into usable, actionable information. This cycle is known as "data to knowledge to action." The graphic below captures the "stack" of elements that constitute AI. It is intended to show all of the areas that are important for ongoing AI research and development, to continue to expand our science and technology.

The foundation is the device and hardware layer that includes powerful computer processing and storage capabilities. The data science kernel layer includes architectures for processing massive amounts of data—essential to managing the explosion of digital data available through the Internet and the growing global network of sensors. The Machine Learning (ML) layer includes algorithms that automate the detection of patterns and gather insights from large data sets far faster than humans could, even in many lifetimes. The modeling layer includes statistical methods and tools for prediction—the ability to move from the recognition of patterns in data to the ability to understand how complex real-world systems and structures behave. We mean "systems" in a general sense: from biological entities, to behaviors, to farms, to cities, to societies, to the cosmos. One example system is triage of inspection of cargo by U.S. Customs. Another is detecting and managing the response to potential false alarms by emergency responders. The decision support layer includes management information systems software that assembles facts, diagnoses status and evaluates potential actions. As an example, decision support applications are vital to enable autonomous vehicles to rapidly react to changing traffic patterns. They are also in use in flexible manufacturing systems in American factories. Decision support capabilities also include tools to detect human emotion and intent and create profiles from the physics of speech. Each of these layers builds on the layers below it.

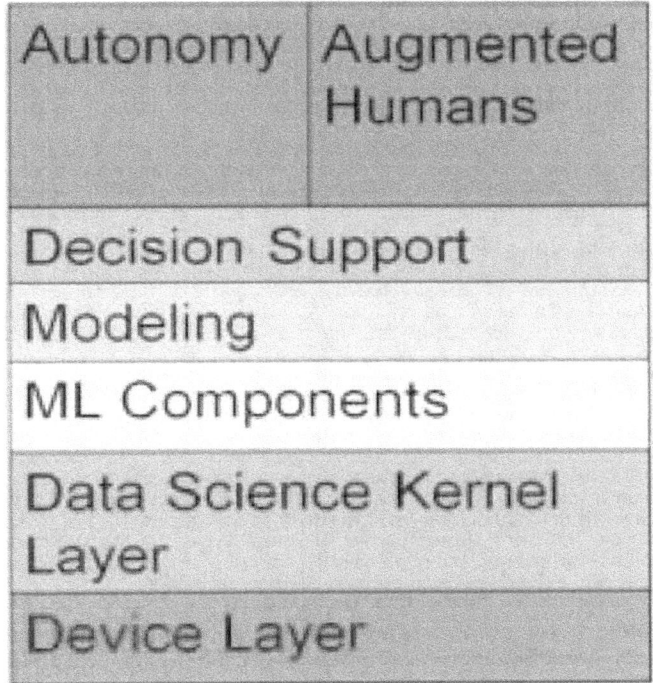

These building block layers power the two major application areas of AI—autonomous systems and capabilities to augment human performance. One application developed by a team of Carnegie Mellon University School of Computer Science researchers, led by Rita Singh, illustrates how the components of the AI "stack" can be applied to dramatically enhance intelligence analysis and crime-solving capabilities of organizations that deal with voice-based crimes.

The world is increasingly communicating through voice: an estimated 700 centuries worth of speech is transmitted over cellphones alone each day. While more people are talking than ever before, even more people are listening. There are 4 billion views of YouTube videos daily. These and other Internet-accessible videos have voice embedded in them. The tremendous outreach of voice today allows for a dangerous world where more and more crimes can be committed and propagated through voice alone. These crimes include those that affect people's personal security, such as harassment, threats, extortion through fraudulent phone calls etc., all the way to societal crimes that affect national security, like hoax calls, criminal propaganda, communication in organized crime, terrorist indoctrination etc.

The CMU team is developing technologies that utilize the power of machine learning and AI to profile people through their voices. They are able to describe the physical appearance of a person, background and demographic facts about the person, and also the person's surroundings entirely from their voice. In recent work with the U.S. Coast Guard Investigative Services, the team analyzed scores of Mayday calls from hoax callers transmitted over national distress channels, and has provided physical descriptions of the perpetrators, and of their location and the equipment used that were sufficiently accurate to enable significant success in the investigative process.

It is noteworthy that the U.S. law enforcement and security agencies as well as first responders are faced with hoax calls on a daily basis, and these collectively cost the Nation billions of dollars in misdirected and misused resources each year. Hoax calls are just one example. The ability to track and describe humans through their voice is useful in several disciplines of national intelligence, where voice is part of the intelligence information gathered.

Our work builds on the fact that humans can make judgments about people from their voices, like their gender, emotional state, their state of health, and many others. The CMU team utilizes powerful AI techniques to achieve super-human capabilities that enable machines to make faster, more accurate, more abundant and deeper assessments of people from their voices. This is made possible by advances in AI, computing, machine learning and other related areas, and over two decades of developments in automatic speech and audio processing capabilities at CMU. The team hopes to be able to build physically accurate holograms of humans from their voices in the future.

This work, and that of many others, demonstrates the power of AI to dramatically help with judgments that humans make and in doing so augment human capabilities. This case is also illustrative of what we at Carnegie Mellon believe will be a dominant pattern of AI deployment: work in close synergy with humans. The nature of work tasks will evolve, potentially dramatically in certain cases, and will demand new and different skills. AI systems that augment and complement human capabilities will help us as individuals and as a nation through this transition and beyond.

Similar examples of AI already touch our daily lives. Smartphone applications that personalize services are based upon AI algorithms. Other AI applications are helping forecast crop yields, analyzing medical samples, and helping deploy police and fire resources. Autonomous systems are at work on city streets, on American farms, and patrolling the sea and air for our national defense.

Intelligent AI systems will also include mobile robots and intelligent processing and decisionmaking among the sensory and actuation capabilities of the "Internet of things." AI systems may always have limitations and will therefore be in a symbiotic/coexistence relationship with humans, and with other AI systems. Designing and building these systems and relationships is a fruitful area for advances.

Perhaps most critically, judgments that humans make in the area of national intelligence are vital to our safety and security. Combined with the wealth of data available today (including through crowdsourcing), AI is the future power source of these decisions—processing far more possibilities and scenarios than humans could alone, and working closely with humans to keep us protected.

And, we are just at the start of this AI revolution.

The Inflection Point and Emerging AI applications and Capabilities

Two specific breakthroughs in the last five years have created the inflection point that makes this hearing so timely and essential. The first is the rapid advancement in digital datasets that are central to AI applications. Current estimates of the world's digital data are approaching 1.3 zettabytes or about 1.3 trillion gigabytes.[4] Fueled by both research and applications, as well as a strong commitment to increasing access to government data, this explosion includes digital biomedical data, mapping data, traffic data, astronomical data, data from sensors monitoring machines and buildings, and data from social media capturing consumer trends from restaurants to travel patterns. Advanced AI applications are catalyzed by the availability of this data.

The second major breakthrough is the development of *deep learning* techniques in machine learning. Deep learning involves a statistical methodology for solving problems in very large and very complex datasets. The term "deep" is derived from the ability of these learning methodologies to automatically generate new models and abstractions of the data. Deep learning brings about the potential for self-learning capabilities that are the central to dramatic advances in AI applications. More critically, deep learning creates the potential for advancing beyond narrow AI—applications focused on one specific task—to general AI that creates a platform for undertaking a wide range of complex tasks and responding in complex environments.

Thoughts on the Policy Implications of the Emerging AI Revolution

The potential transformative impact of these future applications of AI to transform our economy, generate economic opportunity and address critical challenges to our security and quality of life is clear. However, the future—especially the future of U.S. leadership in this area—is not assured. Drawing upon my experiences as a researcher in machine learning, a technology business leader committed to developing AI capabilities, and now as a computer science dean engaging with the aspirations of faculty and students, here are selected thoughts on some of the key elements of a strategy to ensure continued U.S. leadership.

Winning the Talent War

We need a comprehensive set of policies and incentives that addresses the skills needed to win in the AI-driven economy of the 21st Century. These policies must address the talent pipeline, from computer scientists *per se* to the workers impacted by new applications.

The starting point is a recognition that we are already engaged in an international war for talent. Based upon my experience in a leading technology company, a computer science graduate with expert level AI training adds between $5 million and $10 million to the bottom line of a company.

These people are very rare for two reasons. First, they need to have the natural abilities to deal with logic and math and software on a massive scale. Second, they need to survive very intense training that covers many disciplines at once, including algorithms, robotics, security, ethics, advanced probability and human-centered design.

As a result of the rarity of these skills, young AI experts are being heavily competed for around the globe. We see crazy bidding wars taking place from Beijing to Boston to Pittsburgh to Paris. The United States is not winning in the rate of production of these young experts, and we have recommendations below on how to get back on track.

Secondly, AI is one area where international innovation is coming primarily from universities. It is North American professors and their graduate students who have introduced all of the following great advances in AI in recent years: self driving, deep learning, advanced human recognition, emotion detection, provable AI safety, spoken dialog systems, autonomous helicopters, intelligent traffic control, and many others. These have all been taken into the corporate and military worlds through technology transition and through many professors and students transitioning with their technology. The success of AI professors has had great benefit for the economy and security, but it is getting harder and harder to entice new AI geniuses to replenish the ranks of North American professors. The concerns about their retention are twofold: it is increasingly lucrative to abandon an academic position and also increasingly hard to raise funding for university research. These professors are very important because they are the ones producing thousands of AI experts for the country every year. If the U.S. loses many of these professors—and fails to continue the pipeline from graduate school—the supply if U.S. AI experts will dry up.

We will need a balanced set of policies and incentives to ensure that we can provide the talent companies need while securing our long term capacity for research and innovation. This requires recognizing the imperatives of retaining top faculty and supporting graduate students. To support faculty retention we may wish to consider strategies utilized by some of our international competitors who issue competitive "star grants": multi-year awards to the top 100 researchers to enable them and inspire them to continue their academic research careers. To maintain our base of graduate students who are central to our research leadership, consideration should be given to expanding fellowships focused explicitly on AI-related fields and expanding the number of multi-year, broad-based research awards that enable faculty to provide support for students throughout their graduate studies and within ambitious projects.

We also need to move aggressively to build the pipeline of computer science talent. The Every Student Succeeds Act, the ESEA reauthorization passed by this Congress, makes an important start by emphasizing the importance of computer science in STEM education. It is also increasingly vital to foster stronger collaborations across the education spectrum: for example, between research universities and community colleges and between higher education institutions and K–12 to enhance curricula, teacher education, and student engagement.

As has been vital in all periods of discovery and innovation, it is essential that the United States retain its ability to attract the best and brightest talent from around the world to study here, work here, perform world-class research and development here, and start American companies, all of which serve as engines for growth and national prosperity.

For example, Carnegie Mellon is now engaged in a collaboration with Microsoft's TEALS program and Pittsburgh Public Schools to enhance the ability of teachers to introduce computational concepts throughout the curriculum, by drawing on volunteer computer scientists who understand the importance and urgency of computer science education. Similar collaborations are taking place across the Nation. We will need to explore how best to incentivize formal and informal learning initiatives in all communities.

Winning the talent war will also require fundamentally new approaches to workforce training. Many workforce programs tend to focus on shifting individuals to new careers or training workers to operate a specific type of equipment. Neither model is likely to be completely applicable to empower workers to thrive as AI applications impact a wide range of industries.

It will not be necessary for workers to have a computer science degree to thrive in the AI economy. But the capacity and skills to work with advanced machines and understand computational processes will be essential. This will require a mix of technical skills and an understanding of data analytics. This new workforce environment is already taking shape. There are construction firms using advertisements highlighting the opportunity to work alongside robots as a benefit in their efforts to attract skilled workers. Advanced manufacturing is another area that will build on the strength of robotics, while requiring more and more tech-savvy workers.

We have two great resources in creating a skill development environment for the AI era. First, more than in any other period of technological development, we have the power of intentionality. We can advance AI research and innovations with explicit consideration of the human engagement and models of human/machine interaction in mind. It will be vital for workers and workforce development professionals to become integral to the AI research process to realize this opportunity.

Second, the AI revolution itself will give us unprecedented tools for workers to develop new skills. AI is already creating the capacity to personalize training for the individual worker, for example by understanding and modeling each learner's path through a curriculum, and blend technical and academic content that is targeted to the specific job. Combined with innovations like wearable computing devices, entirely new, more powerful approaches to on the job training are being deployed.

Creating a National Framework for AI Research and Innovation

The amazing AI application that describes individuals solely through their voice is built on over 20 years of federally funded research. The next wave of breakthroughs in AI will take place in academic labs, startups and major companies. We will need a national research and innovation framework tailored to this ecosystem.

The starting point is Federal research focused on the critical fundamental gaps impeding AI development. The recent reports prepared by the White House National Science and Technology Council, with extensive input from academic and industry researchers, is an excellent starting point for identifying cross-cutting foundational research areas.[5] As noted in the NSTC reports, we will need to develop a science of safety, dependability, and trust for AI systems. Traditional verification methodologies and approaches are not fully applicable to systems that learn and continually improve. This effort will require both investments in advancing new methodologies and the creation of test beds.

This focus on the science of safety and trust must also include engagement on issues of privacy and the ethics of AI deployment. Through a gift from K&L Gates, Carnegie Mellon University is launching a new initiative focused on ethics, trust, and privacy. Federal support that helps engage computer scientists, social scientists, legal and policy experts, and industry leaders will also be key.

Another critical gap highlighted in the White House reports involves the imperative for continued research focused on systems for human-computer interaction. Research advances will ensure the effective design of AI systems with user friendly interfaces that work seamlessly alongside humans in a variety of settings. Future AI systems must be able to adapt to different challenges, such as providing flexible automation systems that switch from worker to machine operation and systems designed to address situations where the operator is overloaded by the complexity of his or her tasks.

Finally, it will also be critical to invest in the foundational capabilities for scaling AI systems. The most critical need is to collaborate across industry and government to improve access to the knowledge that fuels the capabilities of AI systems. One promising dialogue in this area is well underway. Representatives of agencies, universities, and industry have worked on the development of a collaborative AI infrastructure initiative initially called The Open Knowledge Network (TOkeN). TOkeN would provide a vital core infrastructure for AI development—interfaces to large data and knowledge bases that can accelerate the ability of AI systems to create products and services, broadly speaking, in health care, education, climate and planetary sciences, energy, manufacturing, and a host of other areas. TOkeN would be an open webscale, machine-readable knowledge network aspiring to include every known concept from the world of science, business, medicine, and human affairs—including both raw data and semantic information. The creation of TOkeN would enable the rapid expansion of AI applications for diagnosing disease, designing new products or production processes, and serving our citizens in many other ways.

The collaborators intend that TOkeN, if implemented, would represent the kind of foundational infrastructure that was created to launch the Internet era. In the early 1980s, proprietary, disconnected islands of technology prevented the scaling of applications and services—the Internet connected them. Today, islands of proprietary and disconnected data and knowledge sets are impeding academic research and industry innovation. With a relatively limited investment we can create the foundation for scalable AI development and accelerate innovation.

In addition to a focused research agenda we will need a research framework that recognizes the nonlinear nature of AI innovation. Basic and applied development is taking place in universities, startups, and companies. We need to incentivize collaboration across this ecosystem. The Computing Community Consortium (CCC) has advanced thoughts on how new models of public/private, industry/academic partnerships can be crafted to meet this challenge.[6]

One powerful tool to stimulate this collaboration is Federal support for grand challenges that bring together companies, students, faculty, and often state and local governments to apply innovations to address particular critical societal objectives and opportunities. The DARPA grand challenges have helped advance both the development of autonomous vehicles and automated cyber defense capabilities. AI grand challenges focused on issues such as education, manufacturing, or opportunities to expand economic opportunity in rural areas would have a catalytic impact on both fundamental research and commercial applications.

Align Research and Development with Smart Regulatory and Procurement Initiatives

The development and scaling of AI innovations will demand new regulatory paradigms. Initial positive steps have been undertaken to help advance the deployment of autonomous vehicles but we must summon federal, state, and local, as well as industry and citizen collaboration to craft smart regulations that advance AI and tap its power to more efficiently realize public policy objectives for health and safety. Without progress on regulatory issues AI development will stagnate or, more likely, innovations born in the U.S. will take root abroad, impeding national competitiveness. Combining regulatory experiments and test beds with strategic procurement initiatives to help advance AI products and services will be vital.

We need an "All In" Approach

Synergistic engagement among the Federal Government and our "laboratories of democracy," the states, has been a powerful tool for U.S. science since the efforts to revitalize the competitiveness of the U.S. semiconductor industry in the 1980s. For example, Federal research and commercialization investments in the life sciences have catalyzed billions of dollars of state and local initiatives.[7] These state and local efforts help augment research infrastructure, train workers, expand K–12 curricula, and incubate and nurture startups. Engagement of the states in AI policy is particularly critical as we seek to advance STEM education and workforce training initiatives, foster an innovative regulatory environment, and continually cultivate a vibrant environment for incubating AI startups.

Conclusion

Thank you once again for convening this hearing and for the opportunity to join my distinguished colleagues to share thoughts on the direction and implications of advances in Artificial Intelligence. My experiences as a researcher, business leader, and dean lead me to believe that applications of AI will begin to accelerate rapidly across a host of industries. I believe these applications will expand economic opportunity and contribute to addressing major societal challenges in health care, food production, security and defense, energy, and the environment and education. The "democratizing" power of AI applications to bring new capabilities to individuals on the job, in schools, and in our homes and communities is at the heart of this potential.

My experiences have also made me greatly aware that we are in a global race for talent and innovation. Focused attention on the impact these applications may make on the nature of work in a host of industries and the challenges they bring to our privacy is vital. This will require drawing upon the very best American traditions of collaboration across government, industry and academia.

It will also require research investments to advance innovation in key gap areas that are core to advancing AI and sparking innovation, entrepreneurship and new products and services. We will need an innovative focus on regulatory environments that will be transformed by AI. We must nurture our talent resources: from retaining top researchers, to attracting the best and brightest from across the globe, to creating a national pipeline to nurture students in every community and creative new approaches to support existing workers. I speak with confidence in stating that the university research, education, and industry communities stand ready to engage in helping to ensure that the AI revolution expands opportunities to all Americans.

End Notes and References

1. *Why Artificial Intelligence is the Future of Growth,* Mark Purdy and Paul Daugherty, Accenture, 2016, P.19.

2. See for example the report on research conducted by Forrester, "AI will eliminate 6 percent of jobs in five years, says report," Harriet Taylor, CNBC, September 12, 2016.

3. See American Association for the Advancement of Artificial Intelligence, *http://www.aaai.org/*

4. "World's Internet traffic to surpass one zettabyte in 2016," James Titcomb, The Telegraph, February 4, 2016.

5. *The National Artificial Intelligence Research and Development Strategic Plan,* National Science and Technology Council, Networking and Information Technology Research and Development Subcommittee, October 2016. See pages 16–22, and *Preparing for the Future of Artificial Intelligence,* National Science and Technology Council, Committee on Technology, October, 2016.

6. *The Future of Computing Research: Industry-Academic Collaborations Version 2,* Computing Community Consortium, 2016.

7. For example, in 2001 Pennsylvania committed $2 billion in its tobacco settlement funding allocation to support research by universities and health research institutions, support venture investments in the life sciences and fund regional cluster initiatives. In 2008, Massachusetts committed $1 billion for a 10 year initiative for capital investments in research infrastructure and start-ups. Michigan invested $1 billion in 1999 over 20 years to support the growth of life sciences corridors. For a summary of some of these initiatives and other state efforts see "Successful State Initiatives that Encourage Bioscience Industry Growth," Peter Pellerito, George Goodno, Biotechnology Industry Organization (BIO), 2012.

Senator CRUZ. Thank you, Dr. Moore.
Mr. Brockman.

STATEMENT OF GREG BROCKMAN, CO-FOUNDER AND CHIEF TECHNOLOGY OFFICER, OpenAI

Ranking Member Peters, distinguished members of the Subcommittee, as well as their staff. This is a really important session, and I'm honored to be giving this testimony today.

I'm Greg Brockman, Co-Founder and Chief Technology Officer of OpenAI. OpenAI is a nonprofit AI research company with a billion dollars in funding. Our mission is to build safe, advanced AI technology, and to ensure that its benefits are distributed to everyone. We're chaired by technology executives Sam Altman and Elon Musk.

The U.S. has led essentially all technological breakthroughs of the past 100 years. And they've consistently created new companies, new jobs, and increased American competitiveness in the world. AI has the potential to be our biggest advance yet.

Today, we have a lead, but we don't have a monopoly, when it comes to AI. This year, Chinese teams won the top categories in a Stanford annual image recognition context. South Korea declared a billion-dollar AI fund. Canada actually produced a lot of the technologies that have kicked off the current boom. And they recently announced their own renewed investment into AI.

So, right now I would like to share three key points for how the U.S. can lead in AI:

The first of these is that we need to compete on applications. But, when it comes to basic research, that should be open and collaborative. Today, AI applications are broadening. They're helping farmers decide which fields to seed. They're helping doctors identify cancers. But, the surprising thing is that industry is not just capitalizing on the advances that have been made to date. Companies like Facebook, Google, Microsoft, they're all performing the basic scientific research, the kind of work that you would expect to see just in academia. And they're trying to create the new AI building blocks that can then be assembled into products.

And even more surprisingly, these industrial labs, they're publishing everything that they discover. They are not holding back any secrets. And the reason they do this is because publication allows them to pool their resources to make faster breakthroughs and to attract world-class scientists. Now, these companies, they stay competitive by publishing the basic research, but they don't talk about how they put this stuff together to actually make products, to actually make the things that are going to make dollars for the company. For example, IBM Watson, Microsoft Cortana, there aren't many papers on how those are built. And the thing that's happened is that this openness has concentrated the world's AI research and corresponding commercial value all around the United States. This includes attracting many of the Canadian scientists who really kicked off this AI boom. They're here now. In fact, one of them is one of my cofounders at OpenAI. And, importantly, this has allowed us to define the cultures, the values, and the standards of the global AI community.

Now, this field is moving so quickly that basic research advances tend to find their way into products in months, not years. And so, the government can directly invest in American innovation and economic value by funding basic AI research.

The second thing that we need to do is that we need public measurement and contests. There's really a long history of contests causing major advances in the field. For example, the DARPA Grand Challenge really led directly to the self-driving technology that's being commercialized today. But, really important, as well, measures and contests help distinguish hype from substance, and they offer better forecasting. And so, good policy responses and a healthy public debate are really going to depend on people having clear data about how the technology is progressing. What can we do? What still remains science fiction? How fast are things moving? So, we really support OSTP's recommendation that the government keep a close watch on AI advancement, and that it work with industry to measure it.

The third thing that we need is that we need industry, government, and academia to start coordinating on safety, security, and ethics. The Internet was really built with security as an afterthought. And we're still paying the cost for that today.

With AI, we should consider safety, security, and ethics as early as possible—and that means today—and start baking these into the technologies—into the fundamental building blocks that are being created today.

Academic and industrial participants are already starting to co-ordinate on responsible development of AI. For example, we recently published a paper, together with Stanford, Berkeley, and Google, laying out a roadmap for AI safety research. Now, what would help is feedback from the government about what issues are most concerning to it so that we can start addressing those from as early a date as possible.

As the Chairman said in his opening statement, Accenture recently reported that AI has the potential to double economic growth rates by 2035, which would really make it into the engine for our future economy. The best way to create a good future is to invent it. And we have that opportunity with AI by investing in open, basic research, by creating competitions and measurement, and by coordinating on safety, security, and ethics.

Thank you for your time, and I look forward to the Q&A.

[The prepared statement of Mr. Brockman follows:]

PREPARED STATEMENT OF GREG BROCKMAN, CO-FOUNDER
AND CHIEF TECHNOLOGY OFFICER, OPENAI

Thank you Chairman Cruz, Ranking Member Peters, distinguished members of the Subcommittee. Today's hearing presents an important first opportunity for the members of the Senate to understand and analyze the potential impacts of artificial intelligence on our Nation and the world, and to refine thinking on the best ways in which the U.S. Government might approach AI. I'm honored to have been invited to give this testimony today.

By way of introduction, I'm Greg Brockman, co-founder and Chief Technology Officer of OpenAI. OpenAI is a non-profit AI research company. Our mission is to build safe, advanced AI technology and ensure that its benefits are distributed to everyone. OpenAI is chaired by technology executives Sam Altman and Elon Musk.

The U.S. has led the way in almost all technological breakthroughs of the last hundred years, and we've reaped enormous economic rewards as a result. Currently, we have a lead, but hardly a monopoly, in AI. For instance, this year Chinese teams won the top categories in a Stanford University-led image recognition competition. South Korea has declared a billion dollar AI fund. Canada produced some technologies enabling the current boom, and recently announced an investment into key areas of AI.

I'd like to share 3 key points for how we can best succeed in AI and what the U.S. Government might do to advance this agenda. First, we need to compete on applications, but cooperate on open, basic research. Second, we need to create public measurement and contests. And third, we need to increase coordination between industry and government on safety, security, and ethics.

I. Competition and Cooperation

AI applications are rapidly broadening from what they were just a few years ago: from helping farmers decide which fields to seed, to warehouse robots, to medical diagnostics, certain AI-enabled applications are penetrating and enabling businesses and improving everyday life. These and other applications will create new companies and new jobs that don't exist today—in much the same way that the Internet did. But even discovering the full range of applications requires significant scientific advances. So industry is not just working on applications: companies like Facebook, Google, and Microsoft are performing basic research as well, trying to create the essential AI building blocks which can later be assembled into products.

Perhaps surprisingly, the industry labs are publishing everything they discover. Publication allows them to pool their resources to create faster breakthroughs, and to attract top scientists, most of whom are motivated more by advancing society and improving the future, than personal financial gain.

Companies stay competitive by publishing their basic research, but not the details of their products. The inventor of a technique is usually the first to deploy it, as it has the right in-house infrastructure and expertise. For example, AI techniques developed by Google's subsidiary DeepMind to solve Atari video games were applied to increase the efficiency of Google's own data centers. DeepMind shared their basic techniques by publishing the Atari research papers, but did not share their applied work on data center efficiency.

Openness enables academia and industry to reinforce each other. Andrew Moore of Carnegie Mellon University says it's not unusual that between 10 and 20 percent of the staff he hires will take leaves of absence to work in industry or found a start-up. Pieter Abbeel, a researcher at OpenAI, splits his time between OpenAI and the University of California at Berkeley; likewise, Stanford Professor Fei-Fei Li is spending time at both Stanford and Google; and many other companies and organizations work with academics. This ensures that the private sector is able to master the latest scientific techniques, and that universities are able to understand the problems relevant for industry.

Openness has concentrated the world's AI research activity around the U.S. (including attracting many of the Canadian scientists who helped start the current AI boom), and allowed us to define its culture and values. Foreign firms like China's Baidu have opened U.S.-based research labs and have also started publishing. As AI becomes increasingly useful, the pool of experts we're gathering will be invaluable to ensuring that its economic activity also remains centered on the U.S.

Recommendations—

We recommend the following, to ensure that our basic AI research community remains the strongest in the world:

A. Maintain or increase basic research funding for AI: In 2015, the government's unclassified investment in AI-related technology was approximately $1.1 billion, according to The National Artificial Intelligence Research and Development Strategic Plan report from the National Science and Technology Council.[1] As highlighted by Jason Furman, Chairman of the Council of Economic Advisers, there's evidence that the socially optimal level of funding for basic research is two to four times greater than actual spending.[2] Given that it only takes months for a basic AI advance to result in new companies and products, usually by whoever made the advance, we support increasing funding for basic research in this domain. If we want these breakthroughs to be made in the U.S., we'll need to conduct basic research across a number of subfields of AI, and encourage the community to share their insights with each other. We'll need to allow our academics to freely explore ideas that go against consensus, or whose value has high uncertainty. This is supported by history: companies like Google and Microsoft rely on AI technologies that originated with a small group of maverick academics.

B. Increase the supply of AI academics: Industry has an insatiable demand for people with AI training, which will only increase for the foreseeable future. We need to grow the supply of people trained in AI techniques; this will let us make more research breakthroughs, give industry the people it needs to commercialize the basic science, and train the next generation of scientists. NSF could explore adjusting its policies to allow more competitive salaries for those working on Federal academic grants.

C. Enhance the professional diversity of the AI field: Today, AI consists mostly of individuals with degrees in computer science, mathematics, and neuroscience, with a significant gender bias towards men. As AI increases its societal impact, we need to increase the diversity of professional views within the AI community. Government can explore making more interdisciplinary research grants available to incentivize experts in other fields, such as law or agriculture or philosophy, to work with AI researchers. We also support the White House's Computer Science for All initiative, and the OSTP's recommendation that government should create a Federal workforce with diverse perspectives on AI.

II. The Need For Public Measurement and Contests

Objective measures of progress help government and the public distinguish real progress from hype. It's very easy to sensationalize AI research, but we should remember that advanced AI has seemed just around the corner for decades. Good policy responses and a healthy public debate hinge on people having access to clear data about which parts of the technology are progressing, and how quickly. Given that some AI technologies, such as self-driving cars, have the potential to impact society in a number of significant ways, we support OSTP's recommendation that

---

[1] National Science and Technology Council, Networking and Information Technology Research and Development Subcommittee. 2016. "The National Artificial Intelligence Research and Development Strategic Plan" report: https://www.whitehouse.gov/sites/default/files/whitehouse_files/microsites/ostp/NSTC/national_ai_rd_strategic_plan.pdf

[2] Furman, Jason. 2016. "Is This Time Different? The Opportunities and Challenges of Artificial Intelligence" report: *https://www.whitehouse.gov/sites/default/files/page/files/20160707_cea_ai_furman.pdf*

the government keep a close watch on the advancement of specific AI technologies, and work with industry to measure the progression of the technology.

Also, having a measurable goal for AI technologies helps researchers select which problems to solve. In 2004, DARPA hosted a self-driving car competition along a 150-mile course in the Mojave Desert—the top competitor made it only seven miles. By 2007, DARPA hosted an Urban Challenge to test self-driving cars on a complex, urban environment, and six of the eleven teams completed the course. Today, Uber, Google, Tesla, and others are working on commercializing self-driving car technology.

Similarly, when Fei-Fei Li and her collaborators at Stanford launched the image recognition ImageNet competition in 2010, it was designed to be beyond the capabilities of existing systems. That impossibility gave the world's research community an incentive to develop techniques at the very edge of possibility. In 2012, academics won first place using a neural network-based approach, which proved the value of the technique and kickstarted the current AI boom. The winning ImageNet team formed a startup and were subsequently hired by industry to create new products. One member, Ilya Sutskever, is one of my co-founders at OpenAI, and the other two members work at Google. This shows how competitions can provoke research breakthroughs, and translate into an economic advantage for industry.

We're moving from an era of narrow AI systems to general ones. Narrow AI systems typically do one thing extremely well, like categorize an image, transcribe a speech, or master a computer game. General AI systems will contain suites of different capabilities; they will be able to solve many tasks and improvise new solutions when they run into trouble. They will require new ways to test and benchmark their performance. Measuring the capabilities of these new multi-purpose systems will help government track the technology's progress and respond accordingly.

Recommendations—

Government can create objective data about AI progress in the following ways:

A. Modern competitions: AI systems have often been measured by performance on a static dataset. Modern systems will act in the real world, and their actions will influence their surroundings, so static datasets are a poor way to measure performance. We need competitions which capture more of the complexity of the real world, particularly in developing areas such as robotics, personal assistants, and language understanding. The government can continue designing competitions itself, as DARPA did recently with the Cyber Grand Challenge, or support others who are doing so.

B. Government information gathering: Government should gather information about the AI field as a whole. Researchers tend to focus on advancing the state of the art in one area, but the bigger picture is likely to be crucial for policymakers, and valuable to researchers as well. The government can invest in careful monitoring of the state of the field, forecasting its progress, and predicting the onset of significant AI applications.

III. Increase Coordination Between Industry and Government on Safety, Security, and Ethics

The Internet was built with security as an afterthought, rather than a core principle. We're still paying the cost for that today, with companies such as Target being hacked due to using insecure communication protocols. With AI, we should consider safety, security, and ethics as early as possible, and bake these into the technologies we develop.

Academic and industrial participants are starting to coordinate on responsible development of AI. For example, we recently worked with researchers from Stanford, Berkeley, and Google to lay out a roadmap for safety research in our paper "Concrete Problems in AI Safety."[3] Non-profit groups like the Partnership on AI and OpenAI are forming to ensure that research is done responsibly and beneficially.

Recommendations—

Industry dialog: Government can help the AI community by giving feedback about the what aspects of progress it needs to understand in preparing policy. As the OSTP recommended in its report, Preparing for the future of Artificial Intelligence,[4]

---

[3] Amodei, Dario *et al.,* 2016. "Concrete Problems in AI Safety" research paper: *https://arxiv.org/abs/1606.06565*

[4] Executive Office of the President, National Science and Technology Council Committee on Technology. 2016. "Preparing for the future of artificial intelligence" report: *https://www.whitehouse.gov/sites/default/files/whitehouse_files/microsites/ostp/NSTC/preparing_for_the_future_of_ai.pdf*

the NSTC Subcommittee on Machine Learning and Artificial Intelligence should meet with industry participants to track the progression of AI. OpenAI and our peers can use these meetings to understand what we should monitor in our own work to give government the telemetry needed to calibrate policy responses.

Accenture recently reported that AI has the potential to double economic growth rates by 2035, which would make it the engine for our future economy. Having the most powerful economy in the world will eventually require having the most AI-driven one, and the U.S. accordingly must lead the development and application of AI technologies along the way. The best way to ensure a good future is to invent it.

Thank you for your time and focus on this critical topic. I am pleased to address any questions.

Senator CRUZ. Thank you, Mr. Brockman. And I was encouraged by your testimony about the Canadian scientists coming to this country. And I will say, as someone born in Calgary, that I think there are colleagues of mine on both sides of the aisle who have concerns about Canadians coming to this country.

[Laughter.]

Senator CRUZ. Dr. Chien.

STATEMENT OF DR. STEVE A. CHIEN, TECHNICAL GROUP SUPERVISOR, ARTIFICIAL INTELLIGENCE GROUP, JET PROPULSION LABORATORY, NATIONAL AERONAUTICS AND SPACE ADMINISTRATION

Dr. CHIEN. Chairman Cruz, Ranking Member Peters, and members of the Committee, thank you for this great opportunity to speak to you on this topic of artificial intelligence, and specifically its relationship to space exploration.

For the record, I'm here as an employee of NASA's Jet Propulsion Laboratory, which is a federally-funded research and development center managed by the California Institute of Technology for NASA.

As a Senior Research Scientist in Autonomous Systems at JPL, I work on the development and application of artificial intelligence to NASA's missions. I've had the privilege to lead the deployment of AI software to NASA's Earth Observing I mission, NASA's Mars Exploration Rovers mission and also the European Space Agency's Rosetta mission. We focus on using AI to improve the effectiveness of conducting science and observation activities to—in NASA's missions.

I know of no better introduction to this topic than to point out that, as we speak right now, there's a spacecraft, called Earth Observing I, that's flying about 7,000 kilometers overhead, weighs about 500 kilograms, and is flying at 7 and a half kilometers per second, that is fully under the control of AI software. This spacecraft has been under the control of this AI software for over a dozen years and has successfully acquired over 60,000 images under the control of the software, and issued over 2.6 million commands. The AI software that's used in the operation of this mission includes constraint-based scheduling software to enable the spacecraft to be operated by end users, scientists and people who monitor natural hazards, such as volcanoes and flooding. Onboard software, including machine-learning classifiers, enables the spacecraft to more effectively monitor these science events—again, flooding, volcanism, as well as cryosphere, the freeze and thaw of the Earth's environment.

Furthermore, in a range of collaborations all around the world, this spacecraft has been integrated into a network with other space systems as well as ground sensor networks. And these—the extent of this multi-agent AI system goes as far as Thailand, Iceland, Sicily, Namibia, and even Antarctica. What this system enables us to do is enable data from one part of the system, such as a seismographic sensor at a volcano in Antarctica, to trigger the observation of the system via space assets.

Going even further afield, on Mars, autonomous navigation software is at the heart of all of the Mars Rover exploration missions. And this is, at its core, AI-based search software. AI and computer-vision software form the core of the AEGIS system, which is now operational on both the Mars Exploration Rover mission and the Mars Science Laboratory Rover. AEGIS enables the Rovers to automatically target science measurements based on general science criteria, such as texture, size, shape, and color, without the ground in the loop, dramatically enhancing the science that the Rovers can conduct.

Machine learning has also had significant impact in dealing with the enormous data sets that space missions produce. Just two examples. In the very long baseline array, radio science is being enhanced by machine learning. Machine learning is used to identify millisecond-duration radio transients and reject radio frequency interference events. Here, machine learning allows the automatic triage from thousands of candidates down to tens of candidates for manual review by highly expert scientists.

In visual astronomy, in the Intermediate Palomar Transient Facility, machine learning is applied to identifying transients. Point transients—point source transients are typically supernova, and streaking transients are near-Earth objects. Here, machine learning has been used to perform vast daily triage of millions of candidate events down to tens of events; again, allowing the human experts to focus on the most likely candidates and enhance the science.

While these examples may give you the impression that AI is commonplace in space exploration, I assure you this is not the case. The above examples are a sampling of AI success stories on a small fraction of the overall space missions. Because of the high-stakes nature of space exploration, the adoption of disruptive technologies like AI requires an extensive track record of success as well as continuous contact with the key stakeholders of science, operations, and engineering. However, AI has made tremendous progress in the recent years. Instruments in the Mars 2020 Rover will have unprecedented ability to recognize features and retarget themselves to enhance science. The Mars 2020 Rover mission is also investigating other use of onboard scheduling technologies to best use available Rover resources. And the Europa multi-flyby mission is also investigating the use of onboard autonomy capabilities to achieve science despite Jupiter radiation—the Jupiter radiation environment, which causes processor resets.

In the future, AI will also have applications in the manned program in order to best use scarce astronaut time resources. Past efforts have placed AI in a critical position for future space exploration to increasingly hostile and distant destinations. What we need is sustained resources and a commitment, support, and vision for AI to fulfill its vast potential to revolutionize space exploration.

Thank you very much for your time.

[The prepared statement of Dr. Chien follows:]

PREPARED STATEMENT OF DR. STEVE A. CHIEN, TECHNICAL GROUP SUPERVISOR, ARTIFICIAL INTELLIGENCE GROUP, JET PROPULSION LABORATORY, NATIONAL AERONAUTICS AND SPACE ADMINISTRATION

Chairman Cruz, Ranking Member Peters, and Members of the Committee, thank you for the opportunity to speak to you on this topic of Artificial Intelligence (AI), and specifically it's relation to space exploration.

For the record, I am here as an employee of NASA's Jet Propulsion Laboratory, which is a Federally Funded Research & Development Center, managed by the California Institute of Technology for NASA.

As a Senior Research Scientist specializing in Autonomous Systems at JPL, I work on the development and application of Artificial Intelligence to NASA missions. I have had the privilege to lead the deployment of AI software to NASA's Earth Observing One and Mars Exploration Rovers missions, as well as for European Space Agency's Rosetta mission. Separately, The Artificial Intelligence Group has deployed additional AI software to the Mars Exploration Rovers and Mars Science Laboratory missions, as well as to NASA's Deep Space Network. In my group and related groups at JPL, we focus on using AI to improve the performance of space exploration assets: to conduct more science, improve response to track science phenomena and natural hazards, and increase the efficiency of operations.

I know of no better introduction to this topic than to point out that as we speak, a spacecraft, Earth Observing One, weighing 500 kg, flying at about 7.5 km/s, at about 700km altitude, is operating under the control of Artificial Intelligence software called "The Autonomous Sciencecraft." This software, which has parts both on the spacecraft and in the ground system, has been the primary operations system for this mission for over a dozen years. In this time, the spacecraft has acquired over 60,000 images and issued over 2.6 million commands.

This AI software has improved the efficiency of spacecraft operations using AI constraint-based scheduling technology, enabling direct tasking by end users such as scientists and natural hazard institutions. Additionally, onboard smarts (including AI/Machine Learning classification techniques) are used to detect and track volcanic activity, wildfires, and flooding to enable rapid generation of alerts and summary products. The most advanced of this software uses imaging spectroscopy to discriminate between different substances in images—these techniques have wide applications to environmental monitoring.

Furthermore, in a range of collaborations, this spacecraft has been networked together (via the ground and Internet) in a sensorweb with other spacecraft and ground sensor networks to provide a unique capability to track volcanism, wildfires, and flooding worldwide, with linkages to Thailand, Iceland, Hawaii, Sicily, Namibia, and even Antarctica to name a few. This AI multi-agent system enables detections from one part of the system to automatically trigger targeted observations from another part of the system, as well as enabling autonomous retrieval, analysis, and delivery of relevant data to interested parties.

On Mars, the autonomous navigation software used on all of the Mars rovers has at its core AI-based search software. AI and computer vision software form the core of the Autonomous Exploration for Gathering Increased Science (AEGIS) system, now in operational use on both the Mars Exploration Rover and Mars Science Laboratory Rovers. AEGIS enables the rovers to autonomously target science measurements based on general science criteria such as texture, size, shape, and color without the ground in the loop, thereby improving rover science productivity.

Machine Learning also has significant impact in dealing with the enormous datasets generated in science observatories. Just a few examples follow:

- In the Very Long Baseline Array (VLBA) Fast Radio Transients Experiment (V-FASTR), Machine Learning is used to identify millisecond duration radio transients and reject radio frequency interference in the VLBA. This Machine Learning enables fast triage of order of 10^3 transient candidates daily to 10's of candidates for human review.

- In the Intermediate Palomar Transient Factory (i-PTF), Machine Learning is applied to visual imagery to identify candidate point source (*e.g.,* supernovae) and streaking (*e.g.,* near Earth Asteroids) transients for daily fast triage from order of 10^6 candidates to 10's of candidates for human review.

Significant AI technology is used in the scheduling systems for space missions. These systems enable the operations teams to manage the incredible complexity of spacecraft and science with often thousands to tens of thousands of science and engineering activities and constraints. These systems include SPIKE for Hubble Space Telescope, Spitzer Space Telescope, as well planned use for the James Webb Space Telescope, the MAPGEN use for the Mars Exploration Rovers and LADEE Activity Scheduling System (LASS) for the Lunar Atmospheric Dust Environment Explorer (LADEE) mission. In addition, NASA's Deep Space Network, used for communications to all of the NASA missions beyond Earth Orbit, uses AI scheduling technology.

While these examples may give you the impression that AI is commonplace in space exploration, I assure you that this not the case. The above examples represent a sampling of AI success stories on a small fraction of the overall set of space missions. Because of the high-stakes nature of space exploration, adoption of disruptive technologies like AI requires an extensive track record of success as well as continuous contact with the critical stakeholders of science, operations, and engineering. However, due to both technology advances and increased stakeholder understanding of the great promise of AI, progress has accelerated dramatically in recent years. For example, instruments on the Mars 2020 rover will have unprecedented ability to recognize features and retarget to enhance science. Mars 2020 is also investigating the use of an onboard re-scheduling capability to best use available resources. The Europa Multiple-Flyby mission is studying autonomy capabilities needed to achieve science in the presence of Jovian radiation induced processor resets.

In the future, AI will likely have many applications in human spaceflight missions where astronaut time is at a premium, as well as in robotic missions where the technology may enable missions of increasing complexity and autonomy. Past efforts have placed AI in critical position for future space exploration. Sustained resources, support, and vision are needed for AI to fulfill its vast potential to revolutionize space exploration.

For further information see:

Autonomous Sciencecraft/Earth Observing One
S. Chien, R. Sherwood, D. Tran, B. Cichy, G. Rabideau, R. Castano, A. Davies, D. Mandl, S. Frye, B. Trout, S. Shulman, D. Boyer, "Using Autonomy Flight Software to Improve Science Return on Earth Observing One," *Journal of Aerospace Computing, Information, & Communication,* April 2005, AIAA.

Earth Observing Sensorweb
S. Chien, B. Cichy, A. Davies, D. Tran, G. Rabideau, R. Castano, R. Sherwood, D. Mandl, S. Frye, S. Shulman, J. Jones, S. Grosvenor, "An Autonomous Earth Observing Sensorweb," *IEEE Intelligent Systems,* May–June 2005, pp. 16–24.

S. Chien, J. Doubleday, D. Mclaren, D. Tran, V. Tanpipat, R. Chitradon, S. Boonya-aroonnet, P. Thanapakpawin, D. Mandl. Monitoring flooding in thailand using earth observing one in a sensorweb. IEEE Journal of Selected Topics in Applied Earth Observations and Remote Sensing. 2013 Apr;6(2):291–7.

S. Chien, J. Doubleday, D. Mclaren, A. Davies, D. Tran, V. Tanpipat, S. Akaakara, A. Ratanasuwan, D. Mandl. Space-based Sensorweb monitoring of wildfires in Thailand. In Geoscience and Remote Sensing Symposium (IGARSS), 2011 IEEE International 2011 Jul 24 (pp. 1906–1909). IEEE.

AG Davies, S Chien, R Wright, A Miklius, PR Kyle, M Welsh, JB Johnson, D Tran, SR Schaffer, R Sherwood. Sensor web enables rapid response to volcanic activity. EOS, Transactions American Geophysical Union. 2006 Jan 3;87(1):1–5.

A. G. Davies, S. Chien, J. Doubleday, D. Tran, T. Thordarson, M. Gudmundsson, A. Hoskuldsson, S. Jakobsdottir, R. Wright, D. Mandl, "Observing Iceland's Eyjafjallajökull 2010 Eruptions with the Autonomous NASA Volcano Sensor Web", *Journal of Geophysical Research—Solid Earth,* v. 118, Issue 5, pp. 1936–1956, May 2013.

AEGIS/MER
TA Estlin, BJ Bornstein, DM Gaines, RC Anderson, DR Thompson, M Burl, R Castaño, M Judd. AEGIS automated science targeting for the MER opportunity rover. ACM Transactions on Intelligent Systems and Technology (TIST). 2012 May 1;3(3):50.

AEGIS/MSL *http://www.jpl.nasa.gov/news/news.php?feature=6575*

V–FASTR
D. R. Thompson, K. L. Wagstaff, W. Brisken, A. T. Deller, W. A. Majid, S. J. Tingay, and R. B. Wayth. "Detection of fast radio transients with multiple stations: A case study using the Very Long Baseline Array." The Astrophysical Journal, 735(2), doi: 10.1088/0004–637X/735/2/98, 2011

Impact of ML component:
K. L. Wagstaff, B. Tang, D. R. Thompson, S. Khudikyan, J. Wyngaard, A. T. Deller, D. Palaniswamy, S. J. Tingay, and R. B. Wayth. "A Machine Learning Classifier for Fast Radio Burst Detection at the VLBA." Publications of the Astronomical Society of the Pacific, 128:966(084503), 2016.

Scientific impact:
S. Burke-Spolaor, C. M. Trott, W. F. Brisken, A. T. Deller, W. A. Majid, D. Palaniswamy, D. R. Thompson, S. J. Tingay, K. L. Wagstaff, and R. B. Wayth. "Limits on Fast Radio Bursts from Four Years of the V–FASTR Experiment." The Astrophysical Journal, 826(2), doi:10.3847/0004–637X/826/2/223, 2016.

Intermediate Palomar Transient Facility
F. J. Masci, R. R. Laher, U. D. Rebbapragada, G. B. Doran, A. A. Miller, E. Bellm, M. Kasliwal, E. O. Ofek, J. Surace, D. L. Shupe, C. J. Grillmair, E. Jackson, T. Barlow, L. Yan, Y. Cao, S. B. Cenko, L. J. Storrie-Lombardi, G. Helou, T. A. Prince, and S. R. Kulkarni, The IPAC Image Subtraction and Discovery Pipeline for the intermediate Palomar Transient Factory, Draft manuscript for Publications of the Astronomical Society of the Pacific *https://arxiv.org/abs/1608.01733*

A. Waszczak, T. A. Prince, R. Laher, F. Masci, B. Bue, U. Rebbapragada, T. Barlow, J. Surace, G. Helou, S. Kulkarni, Small near-Earth asteroids in the Palomar Transient Factory survey: A real-time streak-detection system, to appear, Publications of the Astronomical Society of the Pacific. *https://arxiv.org/pdf/1609.08018v1.pdf*

B.D. Bue, K. L. Wagstaff, U. D. Rebbapragada, D. R. Thompson, and B. Tang. Astronomical Data Triage for Rapid Science Return. Proceedings of the Big Data from Space Conference, 2014.

ASPEN–RSSC/Rosetta
S. Chien, G. Rabideau, D. Tran, J. Doubleday. M. Troesch, F. Nespoli, M. Perez Ayucar, M. Costa Sitja, C. Vallat, B. Geiger, N. Altobelli, M. Fernandez, F. Vallejo, R. Andres, M. Kueppers, "Activity-based Scheduling of Science Campaigns for the Rosetta Orbiter," *Invited Talk, Proc. International Joint Conference on Artificial Intelligence (IJCAI 2015)*, Buenos Aires, Argentina. July 2015.

SPIKE/Hubble
MD Johnston, G Miller. Spike: Intelligent scheduling of hubble space telescope observations. Intelligent Scheduling. 1994:391–422.

Spike/JWST
ME Giuliano, R Hawkins, R Rager. A status report on the development of the JWST long range planning system. In Proc. International Workshop on Planning and Scheduling for Space, ESOC, Darmstadt, Germany 2011.

MAPGEN/MER
JL Bresina, AK Jónsson, PH Morris, K Rajan . Activity Planning for the Mars Exploration Rovers. In Proc International Conference on Automated Planning and Scheduling 2005 Jun (pp. 40–49).

MEXAR/Mars Express
A Cesta, G Cortellessa, M Denis, A Donati, S Fratini, A Oddi, N Policella, E Rabenau, J Schulster. Mexar2: AI solves mission planner problems. IEEE Intelligent Systems. 2007 Jul;22(4):12–9.

LASS/LADEE
JL Bresina. Activity Planning for a Lunar Orbital Mission. In AAAI 2015 Jan 25 (pp. 3887–3895).

Spitzer Space Telescope
DS Mittman, R Hawkins. Scheduling Spitzer: The SIRPASS Story, Proc Intl Workshop on Planning and Scheduling for Space, Moffett Field, CA, 2013.

NI–SAR
JR Doubleday. Three petabytes or bust: planning science observations for NISAR. In SPIE Asia-Pacific Remote Sensing 2016 May 2 (pp. 988105–988105). International Society for Optics and Photonics.

Radio Constellation Design
S. Schaffer, A. Branch, S. Chien, S. Broschart, S. Hernandez, K. Belov, J. Lazio, L. Clare, P. Tsao, J. Castillo-Rogez, E. J. Wyatt, Using Operations Scheduling to Optimize Constellation Design, Scheduling and Planning Applications Workshop (Spark), International Conference on Automated Planning and Scheduling, London, UK, June 2016.

Deep Space Network
MD Johnston, D Tran, B Arroyo, S Sorensen, P Tay, B Carruth, A Coffman, M Wallace. Automated Scheduling for NASA's Deep Space Network. AI Magazine. 2014 Dec 22;35(4):7–25.

Manned Program AI
G Aaseng, Techport: Advanced Caution and Warning System Project, *https://techport.nasa.gov/view/32946*

A. Haddock, J. Frank, L. Wang, TechPort: Autonomous Systems and Operations project, *https://techport.nasa.gov/view/32946*

Senator CRUZ. Thank you, Dr. Chien.

And thank you, to each of you, for your testimony.

Let me start with just a broad question to the panel, which is, What are the greatest challenges and opportunities you see for the continued development of AI?

Dr. MOORE. I do think it's very important that we grow our AI workforce quickly. And it's interesting that, in a world where we're actually all concerned about making sure there are more jobs available, there's such a gap here, where we're so short of experts. Frankly, I look at some of the other major players around the world in this area, I see that China, India, and other countries are really pumping out the computer scientists who can form this cohort. So, for me, I would feel much more comfortable if we were graduating hundreds of thousands of AI experts every year from our universities, instead of just thousands.

Dr. HORVITZ. So, let me also complement that work by talking about some technical directions. I mentioned human/computer or human/AI collaboration. And we don't think enough about the human-factor angle in AI. It's not all about automation. Of course, there'll be some interesting automation. We can't have people on Mars, for example, looking at those stones and doing the digging. But, in general, there are incredible opportunities ahead with co-designing systems so they work really well. They're human-aware. They understand human attention. They understand how they can complement human intellect and what people do uniquely, and do well. Understanding how to negotiate, to do a give-and-take, a fluid dialogue in contributions between humans and machines. Lots to be done there, and that includes this piece with explanation, transparency. Many of these answers we get today out of AI systems, the best systems we can build are black-box systems that are opaque to human beings who need to understand to learn how to justify those decisions and how the thinking is done, and to understand the reasoning process, itself. Lots of work to do there.

There's another critical direction with thinking through opportunities to take some of the software we've done in the intellectual cognitive space and enter into the real world of physical innovation, to teach systems to work in physical spaces. Our robotics today are very, very limited. Even our best practices on Mars don't do the kinds of things that people can do easily. And there's a coming renaissance in taking some of our advances in AI and bringing them into the physical space.

Mr. BROCKMAN. So, I believe that the biggest opportunity we have is to continue to move very quickly on the fundamental building blocks, on the fundamental technology. And it really feels like, today, we're kind of in the vacuum-tube era and that the transistor is out there, and that we're building very impressive technologies, but that, this is really just the tip of the iceberg. And I think that the biggest thing to watch out for—I think one of the biggest risks is—that we lose the openness that we have. Today, we can have these conversations, we can measure how the technology is progressing, and we can plan for the future. And I think that we can continue to attract the world's best talent by keeping it open.

Senator CRUZ. So, in the early 2000s, I chaired a series of hearings at the Federal Trade Commission on barriers to e-commerce. And I'd be interested in the panel's opinion. Are there particular legal or regulatory barriers or other barriers to entry that are slowing down or impeding the development of AI?

Dr. HORVITZ. One comment is on—I'll make mention—is on data. With the growth of AI and the importance of data in AI, there has been a growth of a genuine need for innovation with privacy to secure the privacy for individuals. At the same time, there are massive data assets that aren't easily available. We had to negotiate at Microsoft Research to gain access to FAA data to help us build new weather maps for the country based on thousands of planes in flight as we speak. We were helped by the OSTP in getting access to that, but it was not necessarily a simple task. But, there are many data sets like this, and we'd love to see public-sector data sets, especially with privacy-protected, made more available for innovation. At the same time, we—while the NIH requires, on NIH-funded projects, for data to be released as part of the contracts that are made with researchers, it's very difficult to have medical data shared as a part of the fulcrum of innovation. And so, we need to think through HIPAA, altruistic data approaches, where patients donate data, new kinds of programs that let us really maintain patient privacy while gaining access to large amounts of biomedical data.

Dr. MOORE. There are some other areas, such as intelligent braking in cars, where there are some legislative questions which might slow us down. For example, it would be tragic if some lifesaving technology, which would make cars safer, couldn't be released because the legal questions about who is responsible got in the way. What I'm talking about here is, if I, as a software developer, invent a new collision-avoidance system which unambiguously reduces fatalities by a factor of three, but occasionally, unfortunately, 1 in 1,000 times, maybe there's a disaster, there is a difficult question as to how, legislatively, we make sure we're ready for this. So, I can imagine a potential impasse between insurance companies, policymakers, drivers, and car manufacturers, where no one is willing to put lifesaving technology into these systems because it's still ambiguous who has the responsibility for what.

Senator CRUZ. So, one final question. General AI has generated some significant fears and concerns from scientists and innovators, such as Stephen Hawking, Bill Gates, and Elon Musk. Stephen Hawking has stated, "Once humans develop artificial intelligence, it would take off on its own and redesign itself at an ever-increasing rate. Humans, who are limited by slow biological evolution couldn't compete and would be superseded." And Elon Musk has referred to it as, "summoning the demon." How concerned should we be about the prospects of general AI? Or, to ask the question differently, in a nod to Terminator, does anyone know when Skynet goes online?

[Laughter.]

Mr. BROCKMAN. So, my answer to that is that I think that, with artificial intelligence generally, that there are a lot of things that we should be careful about and concerned about and think about security, safety, and ethics today. And so, I think that the kind of general intelligence that people talk about, my 90-percent confidence interval on when that kind of technology could arrive, is between 10 to 100 years. It's not something that we're at all capable of building today. And today we know that there are concrete safety problems that we can be working on. And so, I think that we should be investing in those kinds of questions. And I think that that will help us figure out the right answers for the short, medium, and long term.

Dr. HORVITZ. So, there has been a lot of hyperbole, as you know, stimulated in no small part by Hollywood. Great—these are great themes, and they keep us enamored with interesting possibilities. At the same time, we don't scoff at those kinds of long-term outcomes, and want to seriously reflect and review possibilities, push to the limit some of these proposals about what's possible, and, in advance, proactively work to thwart them, to stay on a healthy, secure path.

My own sense is, these are very, very long-term issues, but that the things we're doing today are actually relevant and interesting, in terms of thinking about how AI systems can grapple with unknown unknowns, how it could secure systems from, for example, modifying themselves, their own objective functions, which is one of the concerns that comes up at times. In some ways, I am happy to see the growth of interest in the long-term future questions, because it raises my confidence that we will track closely and do the best we can when it comes to harnessing AI for the greatest benefits.

Dr. MOORE. I would just add that, at the moment, everything that's going on in the current AI revolution is using AIs which are like idiot savants. They are able to search a space that we've prescribed really efficiently. And it is a matter for future researchers, not something immediate, to imagine these kinds of self-aware, self-reasoning systems. Those would be really, really important to get right. At the moment, the AIs we're building are all to do with immediately answering questions about agriculture, safety, people's health. And the students who are being drawn into it are being drawn into it for these idealistic reasons.

One thing you will notice—and this is actually under the influence of some of the institutions my colleagues have put into place—

is, many places, such as Carnegie Mellon, are actively making eth- ics and responsibility a central part of the curriculum for these AI experts. Because these kids today are building the 21st century. We need them to actually understand the human condition while they're doing it.

Dr. HORVITZ. Just to get a sense for the kinds of things that are going on, this coming spring there's going to be an event where we're inviting—or a group is inviting out people who are imagining the most fearful—feared long-term AI scenarios—call them the Red Team—and we're—then we're inviting out the Blue Team to dis- rupt them in advance, and they're going to come together and bat- tle it out.

Dr. CHIEN. So, I would like to take this chance to circle back to one of your earlier questions and tie that in. You asked, What are the areas that we need to work in? I would say that one of the key areas that we need to work in is better characterization and under- standing the performance of AI systems. And this is something that we have a lot of interest in at NASA, because, in our space missions, we need to, if not prove that they're going to actually per- form within certain bounds, we need to have very strong confidence that they will perform in those bounds, because these are very high-stakes missions. A lot of the applications that people have talked about—healthcare, self-driving cars—these also are high- stakes missions. Before AI can control our critical infrastructure, we need to be confident that it will perform as we want it to per- form. And I think this has been identified before in the OSTP study as a key area of research.

Senator CRUZ. Thank you very much.

Senator Peters.

Senator PETERS. Thank you, Mr. Chairman.

Again, thank you, to our witnesses.

And you're right, Dr. Chien, we have to make sure this performs. I've been very involved in autonomous vehicles and the research that's going on there. And my concern is that we have to make sure the technology gets it right with as few errors as possible, because there's already limited consumer acceptance for letting some ma- chine drive your automobile through a city street. There are all sorts of benefits, which we've talked about, but limited acceptance now. And if you had some sort of catastrophic event in a crash— and there will be some crashes, certainly—it could very well set back the industry dramatically, because of the consumer pushback and the public pushback. So, we have to do this in thoughtful ways, which is why, Dr. Moore, some of the regulatory aspects of this, be- fore you put vehicles on the road, to make sure there's proper safe- ty in place, or we've thought through how we ensure that, is in- credibly important.

My concern with all of this has always been that there's a dis- connect between the speed we're on with public policy versus tech- nology. Right now, we are at a exponential rate when it comes to technology. And even though we have estimates of AI reaching a singularity of some sort from 10 to 100 years—we don't know when that is, although things seem to operate a lot quicker than we an- ticipate. I believe that we didn't think we could beat the expert player in Go for a least a decade, and I think that just occurred a few months ago. So we can't fully anticipate what's happening.

I don't know the speed it will go at, but it will probably be quicker than we anticipate. The one constant in all of this is, when it comes to public policy, that operates at a constant speed. It's called "snail speed." So, it is very slow and cumbersome. If we are not doing it now, we have no chance of trying to catch up to what's happening with the policies, going forward.

I certainly appreciate the comments from several of you that we have to be thinking about this stuff now, in a very thoughtful, comprehensive way, because if we wait, it's going to be too late.

I want to switch gears to the positive aspects that we want to continue to move AI forward. You've mentioned some of the challenges that we have: the gaps that we have to fill. I'd like your perspective on where the Federal Government's role is, in terms of research. Mr. Brockman, you mentioned in your testimony some subfields that need work and some other areas. But, I'd like to ask each of you.

Obviously, private industry is already invested. In my opening comments, I mentioned eight and a half billion dollars in 2015. That number is going to continue to go up. So, private industry is doing an awful lot of this work, including basic research, which, traditionally, has been an area where the Federal Government has supported academic research through grants, but some of that basic research is being done by private industry, as well. So, that's occurring. Not necessarily in other areas. But, are there gaps where you believe the Federal Government—there isn't going to be a private industry group out there investing in some of these gaps that we need to figure out. The Federal involvement will be critical to investing in those kinds of research programs, first to make sure that AI moves forward in a societal beneficial way, but also to understand the time constraints associated with the competition that we face from the Chinese and Koreans and other folks.

Dr. HORVITZ. So, one comment I'll make is that, beyond industry, looking at private sector and public sector, academia, there are groups coming together, so I'll just make a few comments about the new Partnership on AI. The full name is Partnership on AI to Benefit People and Society. And this is a nonprofit organization that was formed by Facebook and Amazon, Google, IBM, and Microsoft coming together, working with nonprofit teams to—with Balance Board and so on, focused around sets of these long-term challenges and shorter-term challenges, with safety-critical systems, ethics, and society, notions of how people and machines work together, and even working to stimulate new kinds of challenges and catalyzing new efforts in AI that might not be done naturally by industry. That's one direction. I'm happy to answer questions about that effort, which is ongoing.

Another couple of comments is that there are places and opportunities where we don't necessarily see industry making deep investments. I would call these application areas that are rich and ripe for AI innovation. How can we solve homelessness, or address homelessness, addiction, related problems in the social science sphere and social challenges sphere? There are some teams in academia right now working hard at applications in this space. Recently at USC, the engineering department joined with the social work department. The social work department, looking at innovative applications of AI and optimization and decisionmaking to new kinds of policies that can address these long-term, hard, insidious problems.

Dr. MOORE. Very good. I could not agree more with what you're describing.

Another example of this phenomenon is, I have two brilliant faculty in the Human-Computer Interaction Institute at Carnegie Mellon who are looking at AI to help people make prosthetic hands easily for folks who have lost their limbs. And, they're struggling to find $50,000 or $100,000 here or there to build these things. At the same time, frankly, my friends from industry will be offering these same faculty $2 million or $3 million startup packages to move into industry. So, I do want to make sure that the folks in academia who are building these things are successful.

Another example is, in the defense world, tools for helping our warfighters or other folks domestically who are putting themselves into danger to save other people. There is so much opportunity to use sensing, robotics, and artificial intelligence planning to save lives there. That's an area where it will take a very long time to grow naturally in the private sector. And we have faculty, and especially students, champing at the bit to work on these kinds of problems.

There's another area, which may sound too theoretical, but I've got to tell you about it, because it's so exciting. The big Internet companies' big search engines are powered by things called knowledge graphs, the underlying set of facts about the world which you can chain together to make inferences. A large group of us from academia and industry, and from some government agencies, want to work to create a public, open, large knowledge graph, which will permit small AI entrepreneurs to tap into the same kind of knowledge of the world that the big Internet companies have at the moment. So, in a manner equivalent to how lots of individual networking systems came together to form the TCIP protocol for the Internet, there's something we can do there.

Finally—and this one is going to sound really abstract—the really good ideas at the moment in machine learning and deep learning came out of mathematics and statistics. Without the fundamental work going on by the mathematicians and statisticians around the world, we wouldn't be where we are. So, statisticians, who are often the heroes in AI, need help to progress their field forward as well.

Mr. BROCKMAN. I have three suggestions. The first of these is basic research. And you mentioned that basic research is happening in industry. But, I think that we just cannot do too much of it, in that we really are at the tip of the iceberg here, and I think that we're just going to find so much value. And that's why the big companies are investing, because they realize that, as many dollars that are being made today, that there's 100X or maybe more increase in the future. And I think that it's really important that the technology is not owned by just one or a few big companies. I think it's really important that the benefits and the technology are owned by us all, as Americans and as the world. And so, I think that the government can really help to ensure that this technology is democratized and that we move faster.

The second is measurement and contests. I think that, for the reasons I mentioned earlier, that it's really important that we track how it's progressing so we can have a good debate. And I think that the government has actually been extremely successful in the past with investing in contests. And so, I think you're creating new measurements or supporting people in industry and academia who are doing the same.

And then the third is safety, security, ethics. I think that's going to take everyone. And I think that we all need to work together. I think that that's going to require making sure that there is funding available for people who want to be thinking about these issues. And I think that's going to feed back into all of the questions of—that everyone's been raising here today.

Senator PETERS. Mr. Brockman, I think I saw that you thought philosophers should be part of that. So—in addition to technologists—I appreciated that. As someone with a Master's in Philosophy, that's good. So, I appreciate that.

Mr. BROCKMAN. It's going to take everyone.

Senator PETERS. Dr. Chien.

Dr. CHIEN. Yes. So, I would echo some of the statements that the other panelists made. They've identified a lot of great topics for the—that really require government—a government role. One that I would emphasize is very basic science questions that relate to NASA's mission. So, how did the universe form? How did the solar system form? How did life come into existence on this planet and other planets? These are actually fundamental questions of science and exploration that we really need to leverage AI to go and explore all these nooks and crannies in the solar system. And if you really want to think far out, in order to embark on an interstellar mission to see if there's extant life at other solar systems. These are different questions that there's no clear financial motive, so there's a clear role for the government, to be able to answer these kinds of basic science questions.

Mr. BROCKMAN. And if I could just add one last thing. So, I believe that the statistic for the amount of government unclassified dollars that went into AI R&D in 2015 was $1.1 billion. And that—as has been mentioned several times—that industry investment is $8 billion. And if this is a technology that's really going to be affecting every American in such a fundamental way, I think that that disparity, I think, is going to be something that we should act to correct.

Senator PETERS. Great. Thank you for your answers. Appreciate it.

Senator CRUZ. Thank you.

Senator Schatz.

STATEMENT OF HON. BRIAN SCHATZ,
U.S. SENATOR FROM HAWAII

Senator SCHATZ. Thank you.

Dr. Moore, you talked mostly about the unambiguously positive potential applications of AI. And we've sort of briefly touched upon the terrifying science fiction possibilities, which I think we're, you know, joking aside, keeping an eyeball on, but that is from 10 to 100 years from now. What I'm interested in is, as Senator Peters mentioned, What are the tough, thorny, short-term public policy and ethical challenges that we're facing right now? Not the possibility that machines will overtake us. Not even the sort of question of long-term unemployment. But, I think about doctrine of war, I think about blackbox algorithms that help with policing, or social work or healthcare. And I'm wondering if you could, maybe just going down the line, starting with Dr. Horvitz, give me an example of a short-term ethical, moral, public policy quandary that is upon us now.

Dr. HORVITZ. Well, for one, I think that we'll be seeing interesting legal tests and precedents set up that define new kinds of frameworks for dealing with things like liability. Who or what is responsible? Manufacturers? The drivers of cars? The people who have signed various documents when cars were purchased? I think that we haven't—things are unsettled in that space, and we'll be seeing lots of interesting work there. And there are some very interesting focused workshops and conferences where people ask these questions.

When it comes to using various AI technologies, going from machine learning for building classifiers that do predictions and that are used to reason about interesting problems like criminal justice challenges. Should this person charged with a crime have to stay in jail in advance of their court date, or can they get out early if they can't pay their bail? They're the systems out there that have been used and critiqued, and it's pretty clear that there is opportunity for looking very carefully at systems that are used in high-stakes situations like this to ensure that there are not implicit biases in those systems, to assure that there's accountability and fairness. And——

Senator SCHATZ. So, long as it's not a government contract, where you're working with a subcontractor, which says, "Our algorithm is proprietary. You're not allowed to—we just spit out our recommendation. That's what you pay us for."

Dr. HORVITZ. Well, that's exactly where I'm going. That's exactly where I'm going. So, the question would be, "What are best practices?" for example, and do we need them when it comes to these kinds of applications? For example, potentially with protecting privacy, should datasets used in these applications be disclosed and disclosable for study and investigation and interrogation by people who want to make sure that they're fair and that there can be trust in these systems? The basic idea here is that many of our datasets have been collected in advance, with assumptions we may not deeply understand, and we don't want our machine-learned applications used in high-stakes applications to be amplifying cultural biases or any kind of biases that was part of the collection process.

Senator SCHATZ. Right.

Why don't we go, very quickly, because I have one final question, but I'd be interested to hear each one of you quickly answer this question.

Dr. MOORE. Very briefly. This AI technology is available to the bad guys, too. It is possible to cheaply set up homemade drones in a bad way. A repressive regime can now use face recognition in a way that they couldn't last year. We need to actually stay ahead. We can't just sit where we are.

Mr. BROCKMAN. So, I'd like to actually build on the bias answer and just say that one thing that concerns me is the lack of diversity in the field, especially as we try to think about, How can we ensure that these systems are going to do the right things for all of us? And if you look at this panel, we're actually, I think, pretty representative of what the current field of AI looks like. And I think that we, the government and industry and academia, need to work together in order to correct that.

Dr. CHIEN. I would echo Eric's comments on—we need to further understand how to characterize the performance of AI systems. Oddly enough, there are analogues, from social science to space science, where we work very heavily. We need to show that the datasets collected by our (NASA) autonomous systems are representative samplings of what you would get if you were not smartly collecting the data. Otherwise, you'll actually come up with different scientific theories and mechanisms for explaining things. These same kinds of techniques apply to making sure that your algorithms are not biased in performing as you wish.

Senator SCHATZ. So, let me just wrap up with this. And I'll ask a question for the record. My question is sort of mechanical. Dr. Horvitz and many of the other testifiers have made at least a brief reference to the ethical quandaries that we are facing, a Blue Team/Red Team. I noted, Mr. Brockman, you made reference to safety, security, and ethics. And it's—it occurs to me that, as this accelerates so fast, that, as you do your conferences, as you have your conversations, you may not be—you may not have fully articulated what kind of system among the AI community you really want to wrestle with these questions, whether it's a public-private partnership, whether it's led by the Federal Government or convened by the Federal Government, but primarily driven by private-sector actors. I don't know. But, it occurs to me, lots of good thinking is occurring. It also occurs to me that maybe it hasn't been fleshed out from a process standpoint. And we can't take it for granted that it's all going to happen organically. But, I will take that question for the record, in the interest of time.

Thank you.

Senator CRUZ. Thank you.

Chairman Thune.

STATEMENT OF HON. JOHN THUNE,
U.S. SENATOR FROM SOUTH DAKOTA

The CHAIRMAN. Thank you, Mr. Chairman, for convening today's Subcommittee hearing on artificial intelligence. This topic complements our last full committee hearing, which explored another nascent technological field: augmented reality.

I'm excited by this topic, because AI has the potential to catapult the United States economy and competitiveness in both the near- and the long-term future. AI presents promising applications in the areas of healthcare, transportation, and agriculture, among others. And I want to thank our witnesses for sharing and highlighting some of those applications today.

The recent report and strategy on AI released by the White House Office of Science and Technology Policy provide Congress with important considerations to weigh as we think about what the appropriate role of government is in this promising field so that we ensure that the United States remains the preeminent place for AI in the global economy. And so, I appreciate, again, the witnesses sharing your insights about what the state-of-the-art is today and where the Nation's leading experts see the applications, moving forward.

I wanted to direct a question, Dr. Horvitz, to you. You mentioned, in your testimony, that new kinds of automation present new attack surfaces for cyberattacks. And I wonder if maybe you could elaborate on what some of those new cybersecurity vulnerabilities might be.

Dr. HORVITZ. Yes. Thanks for the interesting question and framing.

The systems we build that are doing sophisticated tasks in the world often are assembled out of multiple modules or components that have to talk to one another, ending, often, in cyberphysical or astrophysical activity or affecters, like car steering wheels and braking and so on. Every single one of those interfaces presents an opportunity to an attacker to intervene and influence the behavior of a system.

There are also whole new categories of attack. I would be—would have been surprised to learn, 15 years ago, that we were—that the community was talking now about machine-learning attacks. What's a machine-learning attack? The careful injection into a learning system, in a sleuthy manner, potentially, of data that will tend to build a classifier that will do the wrong thing in certain cases. So, that just gives you a sense or a taste for the very different kinds of opportunities that are being presented by the systems we're building now.

We often think about security in classical ways, with verification models and encryption and so on. And these techniques often will apply, but we have to be very careful, as we build these systems, that we're taking—that we're covering all ground and we're thinking through possibilities.

The CHAIRMAN. And, on the flip side of that, how can the use of machine learning enhance security analysts' ability to catch malicious hackers?

Dr. HORVITZ. Yes, it's a great follow-on question, because it's a yes/yes. I mean, there's—look, I mean, we have to be cautious, because the—human beings and humans plus machines can be very creative in how they attack, so there's a long tail of possibilities we have to, sort of, account for. But, there are some very, very promising angles with the use of artificial intelligence and machine learning to detect anomalous patterns of various kinds, with low false-positive rates. That's one of the goals, is to do this well, where you don't call everything strange, because people are always doing different things that are safe, but that seem to be different over time and might seem like a fraudulent event, for example.

So, I think there's a lot of promise. I know that—I'm very excited about some recent projects that I reviewed at Microsoft Research in this space. So, I think it's an exciting direction, indeed.

The CHAIRMAN. Yes.

Dr. MOORE. Speaking as someone who was at an Internet search engine before I was at Carnegie Mellon, this is an area where I would claim that Internet search companies are well ahead of what you're seeing happening in the public sector. There actually are some very good technologies out there for doing machine learning versus machine-learning warfare. So, it's an exciting area which I would like to see grow.

On the bright side, a recent DARPA challenge was about using artificial intelligence to discover vulnerabilities autonomously and using machine learning in other systems, which sounds like a kind of frightening thing. But, (a) it is actually important for our national defense that we have these capabilities; and (b) it is one of the ways in which we can keep ourselves safe, by having our own AIs trying to break into our own systems. So, this is another capability which just wasn't there 2 years ago. Carnegie Mellon, University of Michigan, and plenty other major computer science universities are heavily involved now in using AIs to both try to break and warn us about breakages in our own computer security systems.

The CHAIRMAN. Mr. Moore, just very quickly here because I'm out of time, but could you build a little bit on your written testimony about how the United States can win the AI talent war? In other words, what are the best ways to sustain enough AI talent at universities to conduct basic research and drive innovation while also filling what is a growing demand for AI jobs in the private sector?

Dr. MOORE. I think this begins in middle school. The U.S. Government can really help here if we just help kids in middle school understand that one of the most important and interesting things they can be doing with their lives right now is to learn mathematics so that they can be building these kinds of robots and systems in the future. This is something which needs training. It's not that you need to be a genius. You need to be trained in math from about the age of 13 or 14 onwards, understand that that is even cooler as a career move than going to work in Hollywood. Once we've got the kids' minds in the right place, we can bring them through the university system, scale that up, and then we'll be in good shape.

What I don't want to do is keep us in our current situation, where the talent crunch is being dealt with by this massive bidding war for this small amount of talent. Because that's not sustainable when the other continents are doing such a good job of producing AI experts.

Mr. BROCKMAN. I think one thing that's really important is that we can continue to attract the best AI researchers in the world by having an open basic research community that just draws everyone in. It has been working. And I think that we can grow that and strengthen that community.

The CHAIRMAN. Thank you.

Thank you, Mr. Chairman.

Senator CRUZ. Thank you, Chairman Thune.

Senator Daines.

STATEMENT OF HON. STEVE DAINES,
U.S. SENATOR FROM MONTANA

Senator DAINES. Thank you, Mr. Chairman. And thank you for holding this hearing today. Very timely.

Before I came to the Senate, I used to have a legitimate day job. I was in the technology sector for about a dozen years. And our company had several patents for AI design. We won a national award for AI innovation. That was back in the early 2000s. So, we're not talking about something that's new. It has been around for quite some time.

In the Senate, we often talk about what we need to do to ensure the U.S. maintains leadership, looking at global competitiveness and innovation technology, whether it's broadband, smart cities, medical research. So, I'd like to start my questioning with Mr. Brockman.

Could you expand your testimony about what other countries are doing, in terms of encouraging AI? And a follow-on there would be, What do you see some of the competitive disadvantages that we face right now in our country as it relates to ensuring that we be— maintain global leadership in this important area?

Mr. BROCKMAN. So, in other countries, I think there's a mix. And so for example, you see companies like China's Baidu, who, you know, want to scale up their investment in this field. And the way that they've been doing it is that they've actually opened a U.S.-based research institution, and have joined our research community and are publishing and kind of following our lead. With South Korea, I think that sort of around the same time as the Alpha-Go match, that they announced that they were going to make this billion-dollar investment into AI. And Canada recently has been talking about that they're starting to increase their national funding. And so that's the flavor that you're seeing—both companies and the governments stepping up their investments and trying to make research breakthroughts—because I think everyone sees there's so much activity happening.

And, I'm sorry, I actually missed the second part of the question.

Senator DAINES. Well, just looking at—what do you see as some of the headwinds relates to create competitive disadvantage for our country?

Mr. BROCKMAN. I see. I think that the thing we should be aware of—and so, there's a stat mentioned about the number of Chinese AI papers that are published. And I think that that's actually a true fact, but it's not necessarily the most important fact. The most important fact is, Where do the fundamental breakthroughs come from? Because the thing that happens is, if you are the one who creates the underlying technology, it's like discovering electricity. You're the one who understands everything that went into that, and the papers that get published those are in your language. You really get to set the culture for how people build on top of it because you're probably the one who published the underlying code that people are using. And so, I think that the thing that we need to watch is the question of—for the actual fundamental advances, the capabilities that we just did not have before, but that we have now, where do those come from? And, as long as that's us, then I think we're in really good shape. And so, I think that we need to continue to make sure that that's the case.

Senator DAINES. I want to go back to the point that was brought up earlier on the cyberthreat. In 28 years in the private sector, I never received a letter from the human resource department that said that my information had been hacked, until I became a Federal employee, was elected to the U.S. Congress. And I, like millions of other Federal employees, got a letter from OPM talking about the fact that my information had been hacked. I spend a lot of time working and chatting with some of these very innovative, smaller tech companies that are doing some amazing things as it relates to advancing at the speed of business, relates to protecting our assets. I am concerned—and you mentioned the fact that the Federal Government can lag, is not always leading in that area. And I know it's frustrating, because we have solutions here. We can't sometimes penetrate our own firewall, figuratively speaking, as relates to trying to get—front here, to get our government to move at the speed of business. Because I know when we were—when I was in the cloud computing business, we always—you wanted to make sure you were never on the front page of *The Wall Street Journal* because of a hack. And what that does to valuation of companies has been very obvious in the last few years.

So, what do we need to do to ensure that the best technology, as it's moving so fast right now, is in the hands of our best people who are in the Federal Government? This is not a critique on the people that work in the Federal Government. This is oftentimes the barriers we look up here to ensure that we're protecting our national assets. Who'd like to answer that one?

Mr. BROCKMAN. So—if I may—so, I've actually been extremely impressed with the work that the USDS and OSTP have been doing to solve problems like this. I think it really starts with getting the best technologists in the door and then, secondly, giving them the power and empowering them to make changes within the Federal Government. And so, I think that it really starts with the people, making sure that we're attracting them and making sure that the structures within government exist. And I think that, as long as there's an attitude that's receptive within the agencies or wherever you want to upgrade, I think that that's the best way to get this to happen.

Dr. CHIEN. I'd like to jump in here, also. I think one of the key things is—for the government to be at the forefront, or at least participating in the forefront of technology, there has to be an active interchange in what I would call a vibrant ecosystem that includes multiple kinds of institutions. And I'm very happy to say, in the AI and space arena, there's a large amount of interplay between the commercial sector, between the government sector, between small companies. It seems every week there's another company being started up to do real time space imaging of the Earth for business intelligence. I think that all of this is indicative that there's a good structure with this interchange of information. And I think that's the key to making sure that the government stays in the right location and able to understand and be smart in how it uses this technology.

Senator DAINES. All right. Thank you. I'm out of time.

Thank you, Mr. Chairman.

Senator CRUZ. Thank you, Senator Daines.

I'd like to thank each of our witnesses for coming to this hearing, which I think was informative and productive and will be just the beginning of what I expect to be an ongoing conversation about how to deal with both the challenges and opportunities that artificial intelligence presents.

The hearing record will remain open for 2 weeks. During this time, Senators are asked to submit any questions they might have for the record. And, upon receipt, the witnesses are requested to submit their written answers to the Committee as soon as possible.

Thank you, again, to the witnesses.

And this hearing is adjourned.

[Whereupon, at 3:57 p.m., the hearing was adjourned.]

APPENDIX

November 30, 2016

Hon. TED CRUZ, Chairman,
Hon. GARY PETERS, Ranking Member,
U.S. Senate Committee on Commerce, Science, and Transportation,
Subcommittee on Space, Science, and Competitiveness,
Washington, DC.

RE: HEARING ON "THE DAWN OF ARTIFICIAL INTELLIGENCE"

Dear Chairman Cruz and Ranking Member Peters:

We write to you regarding the upcoming hearing on "The Dawn of Artificial Intelligence."[1] We appreciate your interest in this topic. Artificial Intelligence implicates a wide range of economic, social, and political issues in the United States. As an organization now focused on the impact of Artificial Intelligence on American society, we submit this statement and ask that it be entered into the hearing record.

The Electronic Privacy Information Center ("EPIC") is a public interest research center established more than twenty years ago to focus public attention on emerging civil liberties issues. In recent years, EPIC has opposed government use of "risk-based" profiling,[2] brought attention to the use of proprietary techniques for criminal justice determinations, and litigated several cases on the front lines of AI. In 2014, EPIC sued the U.S. Customs and Border Protection under the Freedom of Information Act ("FOIA") for documents about the use of secret, tools to assign "risk assessments" to U.S. citizens[3] EPIC also sued the Department of Homeland Security under the FPOA seeking documents related to a program that assesses "physiological and behavioral signals" to determine the probability that an individual might commit a crime.[4] Recently, EPIC appealed a Federal Aviation Administration final order for failing to establish privacy rules for commercial drones.[5]

EPIC has come to the conclusion that one of the primary public policy goals for AI must be "Algorithmic Transparency."[6]

The Challenge of AI

There is understandable enthusiasm about new techniques that promise medical breakthroughs, more efficient services, and new scientific outcomes. But there is also reason for caution. Computer scientist Joseph Weizenbaum famously illustrated the limitations of AI in the 1960s with the development of the Eliza program. The

---

[1] U.S. Senate Commerce, Science and Transportation Committee, Subcommittee on Space, Science, and Competitiveness, "The Dawn of Artificial Intelligence," (Nov. 30, 2016), *http://www.commerce.senate.gov/public/index.cfm/hearings?ID=042DC718-9250-44C0-9BFE-E0371AFAEBAB*

[2] EPIC *et al.*, Comments Urging the Department of Homeland Security To (A) Suspend the "Automated Targeting System" As Applied To Individuals, Or In the Alternative, (B) Fully Apply All Privacy Act Safeguards To Any Person Subject To the Automated Targeting System (Dec. 4, 2006), available at *http://epic.org/privacy/pdf/ats_comments.pdf;* EPIC, Comments on Automated Targeting System Notice of Privacy Act System of Records and Notice of Proposed Rulemaking, Docket Nos. DHS–2007–0042 and DHS–2007–0043 (Sept. 5, 2007), available at *http://epic.org/privacy/travel/ats/epic_090507.pdf.* See also, Automated Targeting System, EPIC, *https://epic.org/privacy/travel/ats/.*

[3] EPIC, *EPIC v. CBP (Analytical Framework for Intelligence), https://epic.org/foia/dhs/cbp/afi/*

[4] EPIC, *EPIC v. DHS—FAST Program, https://epic.org/foia/dhs/fast/. See also* the film *Minority Report* (2002)

[5] EPIC, *EPIC v. FAA, https://epic.org/privacy/litigation/apa/faa/drones/.*

[6] EPIC, *Algorithmic Transparency, https://epic.org/algorithmic-transparency/* (last visited Nov. 29, 2016). The web page contains an extensive collection of articles and commentaries by members of the EPIC Advisory Board, leading experts in law, technology, and public policy. More information about the EPIC Advisory Board is available at *https://www.epic.org/epic/advisory_board.html.*

program extracted key phrases and mimicked human dialogue in the manner of non-directional psychotherapy. The user might enter, "I do not feel well today," to which the program would respond, "Why do you not feel well today?" Weizenbaum later argued in *Computer Power and Human Reason* that computers would likely gain enormous computational power but should not replace people because they lack such human qualities and compassion and wisdom.[7]

We face a similar reality today.

The Need for Algorithmic Transparency

Democratic governance is built on principles of procedural fairness and transparency. And accountability is key to decision making. We must know the basis of decisions, whether right or wrong. But as decisions are automated, and we increasingly delegate decisionmaking to techniques we do not fully understand, processes become more opaque and less accountable. It is therefore imperative that algorithmic process be open, provable, and accountable. Arguments that algorithmic transparency is impossible or "too complex" are not reassuring. We must commit to this goal.

It is becoming increasingly clear that Congress must regulate AI to ensure accountability and transparency:

- Algorithms are often used to make adverse decisions about people. Algorithms deny people educational opportunities, employment, housing, insurance, and credit.[8] Many of these decisions are entirely opaque, leaving individuals to wonder whether the decisions were accurate, fair, or even about them.

- Secret algorithms are deployed in the criminal justice system to assess forensic evidence, determine sentences, to even decide guilt or innocence.[9] Several states use proprietary commercial systems, not subject to open government laws, to determine guilt or innocence. The Model Penal Code recommends the implementation of recidivism-based actuarial instruments in sentencing guidelines.[10] But these systems, which defendants have no way to challenge are racially biased, unaccountable, and unreliable for forecasting violent crime.[11]

- Algorithms are used for social control. China's Communist Party is deploying a "social credit" system that assigns to each person government-determined favorability rating. "Infractions such as fare cheating, jaywalking, and violating family-planning rules" would affect a person's rating.[12] Low ratings are also assigned to those who frequent disfavored websites or socialize with others who have low ratings. Citizens with low ratings will have trouble getting loans or government services. Citizens with high rating, assigned by the government, receive preferential treatment across a wide range of programs and activities.

- In the United States, U.S. Customs and Border Protection has used secret analytic tools to assign "risk assessments" to U.S. travelers.[13] These risk assessments, assigned by the U.S. Government to U.S. citizens, raise fundamental questions about government accountability, due process, and fairness. They may also be taking us closer to the Chinese system of social control through AI.

EPIC believes that "Algorithmic Transparency" must be a fundamental principle for all AI-related work.[14] The phrase has both literal and figurative dimensions. In the literal sense, it is often necessary to determine the precise factors that contribute to a decision. If, for example, a government agency considers a factor such as race, gender, or religion to produce an adverse decision, then the decision-making process should be subject to scrutiny and the relevant factors identified.

Some have argued that algorithmic transparency is simply impossible, given the complexity and fluidity of modern processes. But if that is true, there must be some

---

[7] Joseph Weizenbaum, *Computer Power and Human Reason: From Judgment to Calculation* (1976).

[8] Danielle Keats Citron & Frank Pasquale, *The Scored Society: Due Process for Automated Predictions,* 89 Wash. L. Rev. 1 (2014).

[9] EPIC, *Algorithms in the Criminal Justice System, https://epic.org/algorithmic-transparency/crim-justice/* (last visited Nov. 29, 2016).

[10] Model Penal Code: Sentencing § 6B.09 (Am. Law. Inst., Tentative Draft No. 2, 2011).

[11] *See* Julia Angwin *et al., Machine Bias,* ProPublica (May 23, 2016), *https://www.propublica.org/article/machine-bias-risk-assessments-in-criminal-sentencing.*

[12] Josh Chin & Gillian Wong, *China's New Tool for Social Control: A Credit Rating for Everything,* Wall Street J., Nov. 28, 2016, *http://www.wsj.com/articles/chinas-new-tool-for-social-control-a-credit-rating-for-everything-1480351590*

[13] EPIC, *EPIC v. CBP (Analytical Framework for Intelligence), https://epic.org/foia/dhs/cbp/afi/* (last visited Nov. 29, 2016).

[14] EPIC, *At UNESCO, Rotenberg Argues for Algorithmic Transparency* (Dec. 8, 2015), *https://epic.org/2015/12/at-unesco-epics-rotenberg-argu.html.*

way to recapture the purpose of transparency without simply relying on testing inputs and outputs. We have seen recently that it is almost trivial to design programs that evade testing.[15]

In the formulation of European data protection law, which follows from the U.S. Privacy Act of 1974, individuals have a right to access "the logic of the processing" concerning their personal information.[16] That principle is reflected in the transparency of the FICO score, which for many years remained a black box for consumers, making determinations about credit worthiness without any information provided to the customers about how to improve the score.[17]

Building on this core belief in algorithmic transparency, EPIC has urged public attention to four related principles to establish accountability for AI systems:

- "Stop Discrimination by Computer"
- "End Secret Profiling"
- "Open the Code"
- "Bayesian Determinations are not Justice"

The phrases are slogans, but they are also intended to provoke a policy debate and could provide the starting point for public policy for AI. And we would encourage you to consider how these themes could help frame future work by the Committee.

Amending Asimov's Laws of Robotics

In 1942, Isaac Asimov introduced the "Three Laws of Robotics":

1. A robot may not injure a human being or, through inaction, allow a human being to come to harm.
2. A robot must obey the orders given it by human beings except where such orders would conflict with the First Law.
3. A robot must protect its own existence as long as such protection does not conflict with the First or Second Laws.[18]

Asimov's Rules of Robotics remain a staple of science fiction and ethical discourse.[19] But they also emerged in a time when the focus was on the physical ability of robots. In our present world, we have become increasingly aware that it is the accountability of autonomous devices that require the greater emphasis. For example, in seeking to establish privacy safeguards prior to the deployment of commercial drones in the United States,[20] EPIC became aware that drones would have an unprecedented ability to track and monitor individuals in physical space while remaining almost entirely anonymous to humans. Even the registration requirements established by the FAA would be of little practical benefit to an individual confronted by a drone in physical space.[21] Does the drone belong to a hobbyist, a criminal, or the police? Without basic identification information, it would be impossible to make this determination, even as the drone was able to determine the person's identity from a cell phone ID, facial recognition, speech recognition, or gait.[22]

This asymmetry poses a real threat. Along with the growing opacity of automated decision-making, it is the reason we have urged two amendments to Asimov's Laws of Robotics:

---

[15] See Jack Ewing, In '06 Slide Show, a Lesson in How VW Could Cheat, N.Y. Times, Apr. 27, 2016, at A1.

[16] Directive 95/46/EC—The Data Protection Directive, art 15 (1), 1995, http://www.dataprotection.ie/docs/EU-Directive-95-4-9EC-Chapter-2/93.htm.

[17] See Hadley Malcom, Banks Compete on Free Credit Score Offers, USA Today, Jan. 25, 2015, http://www.usatoday.com/story/money/2015/01/25/banks-free-credit-scores/22011803/.

[18] Isaac Asimov, Runaround, Astounding Sci. Fiction, Mar. 1942, at 94.

[19] See, e.g., Michael Idato, Westworld's Producers Talk Artificial Intelligence, Isaac Asimov's Legacy and Rebooting a Cinematic Masterpiece for TV, Sydney Morning Herald, Sept. 29, 2016, http://www.smh.com.au/entertainment/tv-and-radio/westworlds-producers-talk-artificial-intelligence-asimovs-legacy-and-rebooting-a-cinematic-masterpiece-for-tv-20160923-grn2yb.html; George Dvorsky, Why Asimov's Three Laws of Robotics Can't Protect Us, Gizmodo (Mar. 28, 2014), http://io9.gizmodo.com/why-asimovs-three-laws-of-robotics-cant-protect-us-1553665410; TV Tropes, Three-Laws Compliant, http://tvtropes.org/pmwiki/pmwiki.php/Main/ThreeLaws Compliant (last visited Nov. 29, 2016).

[20] EPIC, EPIC v. FAA, https://epic.org/privacy/litigation/apa/faa/drones/ (last visited Nov. 29, 2016).

[21] Operation and Certification of Small Unmanned Aircraft Systems, 81 Fed. Reg. 42,064 (June 28, 2016) (to be codified at 14 CFR Parts 21, 43, 61, 91, 101, 107, 119, 133, and 183).

[22] See, e.g., Jim Giles, Cameras Know You by Your Walk, New Scientist, Sept. 19, 2012, https://www.newscientist.com/article/mg21528835-600-cameras-know-you-by-your-walk/.

- A robot must always reveal the basis of its decision
- A robot must always reveal its actual identity

These insights also may be useful to the Committee as it explores the implications of Artificial Intelligence.

Conclusion

The continued deployment of AI-based systems raises profound issues for democratic countries. As Professor Frank Pasquale has said:

> Black box services are often wondrous to behold, but our black box society has become dangerously unstable, unfair, and unproductive. Neither New York quants nor California engineers can deliver a sound economy or a secure society. Those are the tasks of a citizenry, which can perform its job only as well as it understands the stakes.[23]

We appreciate your interest in this subject and urge the Committee to undertake a comprehensive review of this critical topic.

Sincerely,

MARC ROTENBERG,
EPIC President.

JAMES GRAVES,
EPIC Law and Technology Fellow.

Enclosures
EPIC, "Algorithmic Transparency"

cc: The Honorable John Thune, Chairman, Senate Commerce Committee
The Honorable Bill Nelson, Ranking Member, Senate Commerce Committee

———

ALGORITHMIC TRANSPARENCY: END SECRET PROFILING

Disclose the basis of automated decisionmaking

Top News

- *EPIC Urges Massachusetts High Court to Protect E-mail Privacy:* EPIC has filed an *amicus brief* in the Massachusetts Supreme Judicial Court regarding *e-mail privacy*. At issue is Google's scanning of the e-mail of non-Gmail users. EPIC argued that this is prohibited by the Massachusetts Wiretap Act. EPIC described Google's complex scanning and analysis of private communications, concluding that it was far more invasive than the interception of a telephone communications, prohibited by state law. A Federal court in California recently *ruled* that non-Gmail users may sue Google for violation of the state wiretap law. EPIC has filed many *amicus briefs in Federal and state courts* and participated in the *successful litigation* of a cellphone privacy case before the Massachusetts Judicial Court. The *EPIC State Policy Project* is based in Somerville, Massachusetts. (Oct. 24, 2016)
- *EPIC Promotes "Algorithmic Transparency" at Annual Meeting of Privacy Commissioners:* Speaking at the *38th International Conference of the Data Protection and Privacy Commissioners* in Marrakech, EPIC President Marc Rotenberg highlighted EPIC's recent work on *algorithmic transparency* and also *proposed* two amendments to *Asimov's Rules of Robotics.* Rotenberg cautioned that autonomous devices, such as drones, were gaining the rights of privacy—control over identity and secrecy of thought—that should be available only for people. Rotenberg also highlighted EPIC's recent publication *"Privacy in the Modern Age",* the Data Protection 2016 campaign, and the various publications available at the *EPIC Bookstore.* The *2017 Privacy Commissioners conference* will be held in Hong Kong. (Oct. 20, 2016)

White House Report on the Future of Artificial Intelligence

In May 2016, the White House *announced* a series of workshops and a working group devoted to studying the benefits and risks of AI. The announcement recognized the "array of considerations" raised by AI, including those "in privacy, security, regulation, [and] law." The White House *established* a Subcommittee on Ma-

---

[23] Frank Pasquale, *The Black Box Society: The Secret Algorithms that Control Money and Information* 218 (Harvard University Press 2015).

chine Learning and Artificial Intelligence within the National Science and Technology Council.

Over the next three months, the White House co-hosted a series of four workshops on AI:

- *Legal and Governance Implications of Artificial Intelligence,* May 24, 2016, Seattle, WA
- *Artificial Intelligence for Social Good,* June 7, 2016, in Washington, D.C.
- *Safety and Control for Artificial Intelligence,* June 28, 2016, in Pittsburgh, PA
- *The Social and Economic Implications of Artificial Intelligence Technologies in the Near-Term,* July 7, 2016, in New York City

EPIC Advisory Board members *Jack Balkin, Danah Boyd, Ryan Calo, Danielle Citron, Ed Felten, Ian Kerr, Helen Nissenbaum, Frank Pasquale,* and *Latanya Sweeney* each participated in one or more of the workshops.

The White House Office of Science and Technology *issued* a *Request for Information* in June 2016 *soliciting public input* on the subject of AI. The RFI indicated that the White House was particularly interested in "the legal and governance implications of AI," "the safety and control issues for AI," and "the social and economic implications of AI," among other issues. The White House *received* 161 responses.

On October 12, 2016, The White House *announced* two reports on the impact of Artificial Intelligence on the U.S. economy and related policy concerns: *Preparing for the Future of Artificial Intelligence* and *National Artificial Intelligence Research and Development Strategic Plan.*

Preparing for the Future of Artificial Intelligence surveys the current state of AI, its applications, and emerging challenges for society and public policy. As Deputy U.S. Chief Technology Officer and EPIC Advisory Board member Ed Felten *writes for the White House blog,* the report discusses "how to adapt regulations that affect AI technologies, such as automated vehicles, in a way that encourages innovation while protecting the public" and "how to ensure that AI applications are fair, safe, and governable." The report concludes that "practitioners must ensure that AI-enabled systems are governable; that they are open, transparent, and understandable; that they can work effectively with people; and that their operation will remain consistent with human values and aspirations."

The companion report, *National Artificial Intelligence Research and Development Strategic Plan,* proposes a strategic plan for Federally-funded research and development in AI. The plan identifies seven priorities for federally-funded AI research, including strategies to "understand and address the ethical, legal, and societal implications of AI" and "ensure the safety and security of AI systems."

The day after the reports were released, the White House held a *Frontiers Conference* co-hosted by Carnegie Mellon University and the University of Pittsburgh. Also in October, Wired magazine published an *interview* with President Obama and EPIC Advisory Board member *Joi Ito.*

EPIC's Interest

EPIC has promoted *Algorithmic Transparency* for many years and is has litigated several cases on the front lines of AI. EPIC's cases include:

- *EPIC v. FAA,* which EPIC filed against the Federal Aviation Administration for failing to establish privacy rules for commercial drones
- *EPIC v. CPB,* in which EPIC successfully sued U.S. Customs and Border Protection for documents relating to its use of *secret, analytic tools* to assign "risk assessments" to travelers
- *EPIC v. DHS,* to compel the *Department of Homeland Security* to produce documents related to a *program* that assesses "physiological and behavioral signals" to determine the probability that an individual might commit a crime.

EPIC has also filed amicus briefs supporting in *Cahen v. Toyota* that discusses the risks inherent in connected cars and has filed *comments* on issues of *big data* and algorithmic transparency.

EPIC also has a strong interest in *algorithmic transparency in criminal justice.* Secrecy of the algorithms used to determine guilt or innocence undermines faith in the criminal justice system. In support of algorithmic transparency, EPIC *submitted* FOIA requests to six states to obtain the source code of *"TrueAllele,"* a software product used in DNA forensic analysis. According to *news reports,* law enforcement officials use TrueAllele test results to establish guilt, but individuals accused of crimes are denied access to the source code that produces the results.

Resources

- Kate Crawford and Ryan Calo, *There is a blind spot in AI research* (October 13, 2016).
- *We Robot 2017*
- *We Robot 2016*
- Ryan Calo, A. Michael Froomkin, and Ian Kerr, *Robot Law* (Edward Elgar 2016)
- *EPIC: Algorithms in the Criminal Justice System*
- Alessandro Acquisti, *Why Privacy Matters* (Jun 2013)
- Alessandro Acquisti, Ralph Gross, Fred Stutzman, *Faces of Facebook: Privacy in the Age of Augmented Reality* (Aug. 4, 2011)
- Alessandro Acquisti, *Price Discrimination, Privacy Technologies, and User Acceptance* (2006)
- Steven Aftergood, *"Secret Law and the Threat to Democratic Government,"* Testimony before the Subcommittee on the Constitution of the Committee on the Judiciary, U.S. Senate (Apr. 30, 2008)
- Phil Agre, *Your Face Is Not a Bar Code: Arguments Against Automatic Face Recognition in Public Places*
- Ross Anderson, *The Collection, Linking and Use of Data in Biomedical Research and Health Care: Ethical Issues* (Feb. 2015)
- James Bamford, *The Shadow Factory: The NSA from 9/11 to the Eavesdropping on America* (2009)
- Grayson Barber, *How Transparency Protects Privacy in Government Records* (May 2011) (with Frank L. Corrado)
- Colin Bennett, *Transparent Lives: Surveillance in Canada*
- Danah Boyd, *Networked Privacy* (2012)
- David Burnham, *The Rise of the Computer State* (1983)
- Julie E. Cohen, *Power/play: Discussion of Configuring the Networked Self,* 6 Jerusalem Rev. Legal Stud. 137–149 (2012)
- Julie E. Cohen, Julie E. Cohen, *Configuring the Networked Self: Law, Code, and the Play of Everyday Practice* (New Haven, Conn.: Yale University Press 2012)
- Julie E. Cohen, *Privacy, Visibility, Transparency, and Exposure* (2008)
- Danielle Keats CItron & Frank Pasquale, *The Scored Society: Due Process for Automated Predictions,* 89 Washington Law Review (2014) 1
- Cynthia Dwork & Aaron Roth, *The Algorithmic Foundations of Differential Privacy,* 9(4) Theoretical Computer Science (2014) 211
- David J. Farber & Gerald R Faulhaber, *The Open Internet: A Consumer-Centric Framework*
- Ed Felten, *Algorithms can be more accountable than people,* Freedom to Tinker
- Ed Felten, David G Robinson, Harlan Yu & William P Zeller, *Government Data and the Invisible Hand,* 11 Yale Journal of Law & Technology (2009) 160
- Ed Felten, *CITP Web Privacy and Transparency Conference Panel 2*
- A Michael Froomkin, *The Death of Privacy,* 52 Stanford Law Review (2000) 1461
- Urs Gasser et. al., ed, *Internet Monitor 2014; Reflections on the Digital World* Berkman Center for Internet and Society
- Urs Gasser, *Regulating Search Engines: Taking Stock and Looking Ahead,* 9 YALE J.L. & TECH. 124 (2006)
- Jeff Jonas, *Using Transparency as a Mask,* (Aug. 4, 2010)
- Jeff Jonas & Ann Cavoukian, *Privacy by Design in the Age of Big Data* (Jun. 8, 2010)
- Ian Kerr, *Privacy, Identity and Anonymity* (Sep. 1, 2011)
- Dr Ian Kerr *Prediction, Presumption, Preemption: The Path of Law After the Computational Turn* (Jul. 30, 2011)
- Rebeca MacKinnon, *Where is Microsoft Bing's Transparency Report?* The Guardian (Feb. 14, 2014)
- Frank Pasquale, *The Black Box Society: The Secret Algorithms That Control Money and Information* (Jan. 5, 2015)

57

- Frank Pasquale, *The Scored Society: Due Process for Automated Predictions,* 89 Washington Law Review 1 (2014) (with Danielle Citron)
- Frank Pasquale, *Restoring Transparency to Automated Authority,* 9 Journal on Telecommunications & High Technology Law 235 (2011)
- Frank Pasquale, *Beyond Innovation and Competition: The Need for Qualified Transparency in Internet Intermediaries,* 104 Northwestern University Law Review 105 (2010)
- Frank Pasquale, *Internet Nondiscrimination Principles: Commercial Ethics for Carriers and Search Engines,* 2008 University of Chicago Legal Forum 263 (2008)
- Bruce Schneier, *Accountable Algorithms* (Sep. 21, 2012)
- Latanya Sweeney, *Privacy Enhanced Linking, ACM SIGKDD Explorations* 7(2) (Dec. 2005)
- Tim Wu, *TNR Debate: Too Much Transparency?* New Republic

○